I0472896

HOW TO MAKE THE IRS
AN OFFER THEY CAN'T REFUSE

Learn three steps you must take to handle your tax debt problems, reduce your tax debt and get the IRS "hit men" off your back for good!

By

Juan Carlos Samaniego, EA, **NTPI Fellow®**

Federally Licensed Tax Practitioner

The Godfather of Tax Resolution

Disclaimers

I have tried to recreate events, locales and conversations from my memories of them. In order to maintain their anonymity in some instances I have changed the names of individuals and places, I may have changed some identifying characteristics and details such as physical properties, occupations and places of residence. Although the author and publisher have made every effort to ensure that the information in this book was correct at press time, the author and publisher do not assume and hereby disclaim any liability to any party for any loss, damage, or disruption caused by errors or omissions, whether such errors or omissions result from negligence, accident, or any other cause.

Cover design by illustation
Author photograph by Lavonne Benyola

For permission requests contact:
Juan Carlos Samaniego EA
Tax Debt Consultants LLC
1255 W Colton Ave. Ste. 535
Redlands, CA 92374
(909)570-1103 Fax (909)586-9190
Email: Carlos@TaxDebtConsultant.com

ISBN: 9781071447819

DEDICATION

This book is dedicated to the millions of people that are currently following the "law of Omerta."

I know that you are scared and terrified because you have not filed your tax returns and/or owe the IRS money.

The minute you decided to get help that will be the best day of your life. I know I was there and If you need help I am only a phone call away!

Juan Carlos Samaniego, EA
Federally Authorized Tax Practitioner

REVIEWS

"Having represented taxpayers for over 20 years, Carlos's guide provides you simple, easy instructions to stop hiding from the IRS and begin fixing your problem. Whether you owe taxes or know someone else who does, this guide is an invaluable start to resolving your issue."

– Eric L. Green, Esq. Tax Attorney

"Carlos! This book contains a remarkable amount of information for taxpayers, information rarely presented to them, especially in such a clear, understandable fashion. Folks, read Chapter 9 before hiring any tax pros to help solve your tax problems. Carlos provides important information about how to determine if someone is scamming you or can represent you honestly and ethically. Don't put yourself in worse danger trying to solve your tax problems. Read the Tax Godfather's sage advice."

Review from TaxMama® – Eva Rosenberg, EA

"Carlos Samaniego has been making people's tax problems disappear for years. Now Carlos takes us behind the scenes to learn how he does it, including practical, actionable tips that troubled taxpayers can put to use right away to get relief from painful tax problems. This book is a must-read for anyone struggling with tax debt!"

Andy Frye, Founder & CEO, Pronto Tax School, Inc.

"Carlos, What an AMAZING book! The crazy part is you're like my Godfather! Looking back over the last 12 years of working with you, I can count at least five specific times where you helped me out of challenging situations. The best part really might be your passion for helping others. You really do CARE, and this makes all the difference in the world! Your book and real-world experience have been extremely valuable to me and I'm extremely grateful for your help and friendship!

-Rob Minton, Author, Speaker, Entrepreneur

ACKNOWLEDGMENTS

To my family, none of this would be possible

Elizabeth.
None of this would be possible without your
continued love and support.

Andrew and Bella,
I have never been prouder than to be your Dad

Ernie Madison
"My Godfather"
Thank you so much for changing my life and taking care of
my tax problems, so many years ago and planting that seed.

"A Special Message from the Godfather"

"Carlos has demonstrated himself to be a most honorable individual, family man, and civic leader. As a professional, he presents with enviable ethics, knowledge of is profession and usually personable character and has already made major contributions to his profession as an enrolled Agent.

His own prior "travels" back from very difficult economic hardships and related tax issues has already presented him with a unique opportunity to assist many other individuals with similar "adventures". I have observed him answering that call with honor, and expressing that he believes he now has a perspective most other Enrolled Agents cannot have since he himself needed to rely upon an Enrolled Agent tor resolve his own tax challenges.

Thank you to my mentors, coaches and friends.

Eva "TaxMama® " Rosenberg EA, Jassen Bowman, EA, Diane Kennedy, CPA, Rob Minton, Eric Green, Esq, Michael Mack, Esq, Tom Schrieter, Oscar and Anna Cervantes You all had a huge impact on my career and mindset through you books, coaching and friendship way bigger than you know.

YOU ARE ENTITLED TO A **FREE 30-MINUTE TAX DEBT ANALYSIS($197 Value)** FOR PURCHASING THIS BOOK.

If you are reading this book, either know someone that has a tax problem or you are the one dealing with the tax problem

You are about to read my personal journey of not filing my own tax returns for 8-years and owing thousands of dollars in back taxes. In these pages I will describe what happen to me and how I went from having a tax problems to helping people with tax problems.

You may be worried about going to jail, a family member finding out about you not filing and paying taxes. You are not sleeping, you health is being affected, your financial life is not where you want it to be, because of this tax problem.

I can personally guarantee to you one thing. They day you pick up the phone and make a decision to do something about it will be the best feeling in the world. I remember when my "godfather" told me, "you got nothing to worry about anymore. I am going to take care of this for you!"

WOW! That was the first night I got a full night sleep.

All you to do to claim this offer is go directly to my website: TaxDebtConsultant.com and book you completely confidential go to **MeetWithTaxGodfather.com** or call me directly **909-570-1103**. If I don't answer just leave me a message that you read my book and would like to book a Tax Debt Analysis.

Forward

Today I am a tax lawyer. Thirty years ago I was a criminal prosecutor working for the Department of Justice in the Consumer Fraud Division. I was blessed to work with some true champions of justice, professionals who were smart, dedicated, and sincerely passionate about the welfare of other people. It's difficult to find professionals like that, today more than ever.

Yet Carlos Samaniego is one of those professionals. He is truly a champion of justice. From the moment I met Carlos over 15 years ago when our professional paths crossed when he was helping protect credit and debt challenged consumers, to the present as he helps taxpayers escape their tax nightmares, his singular focus is to help others. Indeed, Carlos is driven by a purpose bigger than himself. He is special.

I think a big part of Carlos' drive to help others derives from his own life experiences. He comes from a humble background. He has succeeded on his own. He has raised a beautiful family with one son serving our country in the United States Naval Academy. And Carlos has experienced some of the same financial hardships that many of you are facing. These life experiences shape people, and they have shaped Carlos into the man and professional he is today.

So, when Carlos says, "I know how you feel," he really does know how you feel! When he sees a person experiencing the stress and pain of financial difficulty, he sees himself. He knows what it's like to lie awake at night and stare at the ceiling, worried sick. In a world filled with phonies, liars and fraudsters who are only out to make a buck with little or no regard for whether they are helping others, Carlos is different. He knows you. He is like you. He cares deeply.

And that is obvious in how he practices tax problem solving. I'm amazed at how much the man knows about tax problem solving! He seems to live and breathe the Tax Code and Internal Revenue Manual. And this book is a reflection of the man's knowledge and expertise. And yet this book is also easy to understand and offers real hope for folks who feel hopeless. As Carlos will tell you, there is no such thing as a hopeless tax case. And he proves that every day with how he goes about solving the toughest tax cases that other tax professionals shy away from.

A wise tax lawyer once told me, "If you get the right professional on your side, any tax case can be solved." And Carlos is the right professional to have on your side. And this is the right book to help you begin to understand the proven yet overlooked tax solutions that exist. This book will give you hope. Real hope through real solutions.

Now, this book is not offered as legal advice, and it's not a replacement for hiring a tax professional, yet it is a valuable starting point to end your tax nightmare once and for all so you can enjoy your family, sleep at night, and get your life back.

I am privileged to call Carlos my friend and colleague. I am honored to have had this opportunity to write these words about Carlos and this fantastic book. You can see that I am sincere in my praise. So, do yourself a favor and read this book. Or call Carlos and let him explain in plain talk the tax solutions available to you. You will not find a more sincere, caring and top notch tax professional than Carlos Samaniego.

God bless you
Micheal Mack, Esq.

TABLE OF CONTENTS

INTRODUCTION

If you owe money to the IRS, then this book is for you.

Whether you're going to tackle the problem yourself, or just want to have a better understanding of what your professional representative is doing (or, unfortunately, sometimes *not* doing), this book is your guide to understanding the whole process.

My name is Juan Carlos Samaniego. How I became the Godfather of Tax Resolution began when I was just nineteen or twenty years old. I was an Emergency Medical Technician (EMT), working with Mercy Ambulance, saving people's physical lives in ambulances. I worked there for over eleven years.

Now I save people's financial lives.

After a few years as an EMT, along about 2002, an older guy, a paramedic, gave me some really bad advice. It was towards the holiday season, and lots of guys were working overtime to make extra money for the holidays. He told me if I wanted a bigger paycheck, I should claim all kinds of exemptions on my W2s. So

I did. I claimed about ten exemptions, and sure enough, my paycheck swelled.

The problem was, when tax time came, I owed some money, which I couldn't pay. At the same time, I liked my nice new lifestyle so much, I didn't want to let it go, so I didn't change the exemptions I was taking. In fact, I bought myself a brand new truck, got a nicer apartment, and I was having a heck of a good time with the extra money on my paychecks.

Pretty soon, I just stopped filing my taxes, because finding out how much I owed each year was just an impossible financial burden. I went for years without filing any taxes– almost eight years!

Strangely enough, the IRS did not contact me (I moved around a lot in my twenties). I lived with fear for a while. I think most Americans fear the IRS, but if you have any tax issues that aren't cleared up, you know what fear is! You live under a cloud. You look for that envelope in the mail with the IRS on the return address. Your heart jumps into your throat when those scam artists–even though you know they are scam artists!–call you and say they are from the IRS and you'd better pay up now or the sheriff is coming to take you away. (The IRS doesn't call people without a mailed heads up, so breathe easy on that one!)

You know what I mean, though. The IRS is one of the most feared and hated institutions in the world.

After a long time of no consequences, no letters, no requests for tax returns, I forgot about my snarled up tax situation and my mountain of debt to the IRS. I had a nice lifestyle, I had met my soon-to-be wife (whom I hadn't told about my tax history). I was happy.

Then I got caught. It wasn't the IRS that caught me. It was the state of California, because, of course, I also hadn't filed or paid any taxes with them. They not only wanted backed up state taxes from me, they also reported my situation to the IRS, as they are supposed to do by law. So the net fell over my head. I was trapped!

I was no longer an EMT at this time. I was a mortgage officer in the real estate industry. The letters started coming all right, and from the IRS as well as the state of California. I owed a massive amount of tax debt.

Now there are only three kinds of people who can help you when you are up to your eyebrows in tax debt: Certified Public Accountants (CPAs), attorneys, or Enrolled Agents (EAs). You have to pick one of those three to get out of the mess you're in.

Enrolled Agents are licensed by the Department of the Treasury. The qualifications are to work for the IRS for five years or else take a grueling test. EAs know their stuff, and they are authorized to represent taxpayers in front of the IRS on all levels. An Enrolled Agent is the highest award or certification given by the

IRS, and the EA designation is recognized in all fifty states. It sounded to me like an EA was just the kind of person I needed!

I came upon some information about a guy named Ernie who was local and an EA. Thus I met my godfather! He was a godfather to me as well as to many other people. That's why I can recommend that an EA is going to be a lot of help to you if you are living under the cold shadow of the IRS.

My EA, Ernie, was an older gentleman. When I went to his house, I thought I'd stepped into the lair of an old-time hippie. He had long, grey hair tied back in a ponytail–not exactly your standard-issue IRS guy. Not by a long shot. Plus, he was wearing an ugly Christmas sweater–a yucky green color with Santa Clauses on it.

When I explained my situation to him, he said, to me, "You know what Carlos? You have nothing to worry about because I'm going to take care of you. We're going to get this resolved because you want to get right with the government." That was the most important part: just breaking my silence and wanting to do something about it.

Ernie was so reassuring! He knew what we needed to do. He thought it could be resolved. He had knowledge and power. He knew the IRS's ways and secrets. He had the keys to my prison of fear and had just let me out!

4

I felt like the weight of the world had been lifted from my shoulders. The relief was like breathing deeply for the first time in years! My muscles relaxed, my gut's knot got untied, and I finally thought I could actually have freedom and peace in my life.

And I did. Ernie got that for me. He took care of me. He took care of my situation. I didn't go to prison or have liens put on my property or have my bank accounts drained, or have to pay exorbitant amounts each month that kept me in financial slavery the rest of my life--all the stuff we fear the IRS will do to us when we owe them. Ernie worked out a reasonable plan for me, and we got it done.

That was fifteen years ago, and guess what? The moment I saw what someone like Ernie could do for someone who was suffering like I was, I guess my EMT training kicked in or something because I wanted to do the same thing for others. I wanted to save other people from the burden of tax debt too.

At one point, when I realized there was one more tax return I had missed filing, I remember saying, "You know what? I'm just going to do that right away," because I knew Ernie needed it. I remember just sitting down, doing the research to be able to get that tax return done instead of giving it to my CPA and giving that to Ernie. Then he said, "Wow, you did this tax return yourself?" This was the second triggering event for me to want to become an enrolled agent someday. He said, "You did a really good job. I think you would be really good at this type of business." That planted another seed for me to become an Enrolled Agent.

So I became an Enrolled Agent myself. Ernie was so happy and proud! In fact, we became close friends. He was moving toward retirement by that time, so he referred clients to me.

I could now lift that incredible mental and emotional burden from people's shoulders as they lived with the guilt, shame, and fear as they hid from the IRS, not telling anyone but knowing that the day of horrible reckoning could come at any moment. When clients come to my office, I sit down with them, and they tell me their problems, sometimes for the very first time, sometimes problems they haven't shared with their own families. I tell them, "Once you've come to me, once I'm on your case, I don't want you to worry because I'm going to take care of your problems. We're going to get this resolved and get you back right with the government." I'm the Godfather of Tax Resolution now.

WHAT A GODFATHER DOES

The reason I say that Ernie was the godfather to me was because it reminded me of Don Corleone in the book and movie *The Godfather*. When no one else can help, Don Corleone, the Godfather, steps in.

Remember that first scene in *The Godfather*? Poor Amerigo Bonasera is in court waiting for the guys who assaulted his daughter to get theirs at the hands of the justice system. Right away, though, Bonasera feels like something fake is going on (it turns out he's right–Don Corleone tells him one of the perps has a powerful politician for a dad). Even though the judge rebukes the young men harshly, he does distinguish the fact that they didn't actually rape the poor girl. The judge also takes into account the fact that the guys had clean records, good families, and because of their youth, he sentences them to three years in prison but suspends the sentence. The guys walk, in other words.

Bonasera can't believe it. Maybe the guys didn't rape his daughter, but they did try to, and they did break her jaw and nose and blacken both her eyes. She was in the hospital this moment because of the beating.

"For justice, we must go on our knees to Don Corleone," he decides.

For justice, you have to go to the Godfather.

Now Bonasera had avoided going to the Godfather because he didn't want to pay the price he would have to once he got into the Godfather's debt. He was a law-abiding citizen, after all. But since only the Godfather had the power to punish these perps properly, Bonasera no longer had a choice.

The Godfather carries out the revenge scientifically. He sends people who know just what to do. He doesn't want anyone who gets too excited at the smell of blood and can't stop punching. The guys he sends turn those punk kids into pulps, but, like Bonasera's daughter, they live. Like her, though, they are going to need plastic surgery and be in the hospital for months.

The Godfather's justice is exact.

Bonasera is in a sweat, feeling pretty sure he will be asked to dispose of a body illegally to pay back the Godfather (he is an undertaker). Yet there is poetic justice at work. When it's payback time, the Godfather asks something highly appropriate. He asks Bonasera to employ his great arts to make the Godfather's bullet-ridden son look presentable to his mother at his funeral. Another crime family had carried out a hit on Sonny Corleone. It is almost a parent-to-parent moment when fathers share their grief and help each other get over what others did to their children.

The Godfather is the neighborhood fixer. When the arm of the law won't stretch down to help the powerless, Don Corleone's will.

I am the Godfather of tax resolution. Don't hesitate to come to me. I can help you, and my fee will be fair, just like the Godfather's was.

Your tax problems can be solved. I know it; I've done it time and time again, with cases probably much worse than yours!

You can get this taken care of. All you need is the Godfather in your corner.

NO OMERTA!

The Mafia has this law—the law of *omerta*. That means silence. You do not talk about the Mafia, you do not talk about any of the Mafia's members or their activities or even their existence. On pain of death, as Shakespeare said! You're going to get into major hot water with the mob if you open your trap about them or anything they are doing.

But the law of omerta shouldn't apply with your taxes or your relationship with the IRS! In fact, nothing will work against you more! The IRS isn't going to put you in jail for failing to pay your taxes. But hiding—not filing—acting like they and you don't even exist—that has the potential to land you in jail!

Listen, I know how it is. As I've said, I hadn't even told my wife-to-be about my tax situation. I didn't tell anyone! Maybe I was ashamed. Maybe I was afraid that someone would "rat" me out if I told (to use another Mafia term!). Maybe it was just too terrible to even think about, let alone talk about.

You'd be amazed, though, how many people don't even open letters they get from the IRS! It's like they think the law of omerta will protect them from this powerful government agency.

Well, it won't. Sooner or later, they will find you.

NO OMERTA!

Don't live in silence, all the while knowing there's a great, big, sharp axe hanging over your head, held by a thread. That's no way to live!

Forget the law of omerta, but do get a godfather on your side. Break your silence and there are only three types of people that are allowed to represent you a CPA, Attorney or an EA(Enrolled Agent). Go talk to someone, like I did years ago. Remember, I've been there and done that, so I'm not likely to judge you! What's more, every EA I know has heard stories much worse and more irresponsible than anything you've done or not done! Don't worry! It's common. This stuff happens all the time. You're not alone!

So break the law of omerta, get your head out of the sand, and face your problem. Just don't do it alone. Do it with someone who is used to dealing with the IRS and who knows all their trade secrets and ins and outs.

I will never counsel you to cheat or do anything illegal. But if you know how the IRS operates and what they are really interested in, if you know all the laws and regulations, you know what your options are in resolving your tax problems.

Dealing with the IRS *is* scary, but it doesn't have to be. All you need is a godfather.

Chapter 1

OVERVIEW OF THE IRS AND
YOUR RIGHTS AS A TAXPAYER

The IRS is not exactly everyone's favorite teddy bear. In fact, it's one of the most feared institutions on earth. That's because it has a lot of collecting (enforcement) clout.

Have you ever seen the movie *The Pursuit of Happyness* with Will Smith? The poor guy is living in homeless shelters with his young son, and even spending some nights locked up with him in train station bathrooms so they can be warm and safe. He finally gets a break and makes about $600. He and his kid can eat! They can stay in a hotel room!

The next day, he finds his bank account empty. The IRS drained it for back taxes. Back to the homeless shelter, public bathrooms, and hunger--with his five-year-old son!

Is there a kinder, gentler IRS these days? Well, somewhat, yes. The new mission statement of the IRS is as follows:

"Provide America's taxpayers top quality service by helping them understand and meet their tax responsibilities and by applying the tax law with integrity and fairness to all."

Now, isn't that nice? It's better than their old mission statement, which said:

"The purpose of the Internal Revenue Service is to collect the proper amount of tax revenue at the least cost; serve the public by continually improving the quality of our products and services; and perform in a manner warranting the highest degree of public confidence in our integrity, efficiency and fairness."

Their old mission statement made it look like all they were interested in was money! Of course, they were. They still are. They are a money-collecting agency. The IRS is there to get the tax money you owe, and it can do some pretty nasty things to you if you don't pay up (See Chapter 5).

That's why you need a godfather!

The IRS has a good pedigree. It was founded by Abraham Lincoln in 1862 to raise money for the Civil War. It's a bureau of the Department of the Treasury, and it is very good at what it does. Like many government departments, though, it has been downsized. This has led to fewer audits over the years due to

14

shrinking staff and budget. That doesn't mean taxpayers should not do everything they can to keep their tax returns up to date and above-board, though.

In fact, one of the first things I will tell you as your godfather is that you need to get into compliance with the IRS. You may not like to hear that, but it is the most crucial first step of tax resolution.

Much as we may dislike paying taxes, we all have to admit that we appreciate the services those taxes fund. After all, we want functioning armed forces, don't we? Most of us like and are going to depend at least in part on Social Security. We love our national parks, and we want good infrastructure for our highways and byways. All that and a lot more comes from taxes.

Now, the IRS is powerful, but it isn't all-powerful, and you have certain rights as a taxpayer. You may not be aware of these rights, but you do have them. In fact, you have a Taxpayer's Bill of Rights, which includes the right to be informed, to receive quality service, to pay no more than your fair share or correct amount of taxes, to challenge the IRS and to be listened to when you do so, to appeal an IRS decision in an independent forum, the right to finality (for things to get done and ended in a timely way), the right to privacy, confidentiality, a lawyer, and to a fair and just tax system.

There is also an independent section of the IRS known as the IRS Taxpayer Advocate Service (TAS). You can request help from this service. An independent, local taxpayer advocate can become your voice at the IRS.

So can an Enrolled Agent. An EA has unlimited rights to represent you before the IRS at all levels. An EA is like a godfather.

No Omerta!

Once again, let me emphasize that pretending your tax problem doesn't exist, won't make it go away. Don't throw away or stow away letters from the IRS! Get professional help for resolving a tax problem, and you will experience the relief and joy that comes from knowing you've got a godfather in your corner who will help you address your problems with this most powerful agency, the IRS.

Chapter 2

THREE CRUCIAL STEPS TO RESOLVE YOUR TAX DEBTS

I tell all my clients there are basically three steps involved to handle a tax problem. Those three steps are:

Step 1.) A three-part assessment and strategy: a.) investigation of liability and b.) discovery, and c.) game plan

Step 2.) Compliance. Before the IRS will work with you, you have to be compliant. I'll get into details on what compliance is

Step 3.) The tax resolution portion

We can't even consider resolving a tax issue until you're compliant, but you can't become compliant unless we know what the problem is.

It's very similar to if somebody's sick or ill and they go to the doctor. You don't walk into the doctor and say, "Hey, can you give me some medicine," or "Can you give me a treatment plan for my illness?" They don't know what's going on. So what do they do? They go through three steps: Step one is do some lab test and interviews. They gather information to make a diagnosis. Step two is probably to get you ready for your treatment plan. Then step three is the actual treatment plan. That's the resolution part.

It's very similar to resolving your taxes! So let's go ahead and get started.

STEP 1

When it comes down to the investigation of liability, which includes discovery and a game plan, here's what we do. The initial process of investigation liability literally starts at that first interview. A lot of times people will come into my office for that initial consult, and it becomes the investigation of liability.

I say, "Tell me what's the problem, what's going on, what has you here in my office." Normally we tend to see is people who are in a situation that the IRS has issued garnishments against their paychecks or levies against their bank accounts. They probably haven't filed their tax returns in years, like what happened with me. They are getting letters from the IRS and/or the state, and a lot of times those letters are even unopened.

During the interview process, I find out what's going on. That initial interview is so important because I want to know what caused the tax problem. What caused you to get into the challenging situation you are in? A lot of times there was a major illness, a death in the family, there was a gambling problem, or a whole host of things could have happened. In my case, I ended up changing my W2 exemptions to ten so that I could cover my bills better and have a better lifestyle. I got myself in trouble because I never changed it back. So what caused those challenges? I wasn't really making enough money to support a better lifestyle, so I opted to get more every paycheck.

The reason I really need to know all this and to dive deep into it is because we are potentially able to remove thousands, if not tens of thousands of dollars of penalties, based on what I'm hearing from you. Obviously, we have to provide evidence based on whatever happened: if you were sick or your spouse passed away or something like that, and that caused you to kind of get you into the situation. If so, there's potential for penalty abatements, so I need to know your story.

Once I've gotten that story, if we decide to move forward, if I decide to work with you, what I end up doing is getting power of attorney for the client. With power of attorney, I'm able to go pull all the IRS wage and income transcripts. Those are the documents of W2s or 1099s, so we can see everything the IRS has on you. I can see if the IRS believes that you're compliant or you're not compliant, and if you're not compliant, why you aren't.

A lot of times I get people that come into my office and say, "I haven't filed my taxes in the last three or four years," but when I pull the transcripts, we find out there are tax returns missing from years earlier that they had forgotten.

A lot of people will go to a tax preparer and talk about those three or four years. They start preparing those three to four years only to find out later that they had other missing tax returns. So we get to deal with that. That's why being able to pull all of the IRS records to find out what's going on is extremely important.

Now, one of the things I'm looking for is if you have hired other tax professionals to try to handle these problems and what happened. If you've been audited, I want to know what happened during the audit. Depending on your situation, I might even do a Freedom of Information Act request, which gives me the ability even to pull notes that an IRS agent or revenue officer has about the case. We literally find out everything that's going on. It is very similar to a court case, the first phase that is called discovery, where the other party has to give us all their notes. We can actually get that information. It all depends on the client's particular situation.

Once I've gotten the information from the initial interview, I'm able to pull up all that information, to find out what the IRS has, and what returns are available. When I do a transcript analysis and report, they tend to be 30 to 40 pages long by the time we're done collecting all the information and putting it together. Literally! From all that information, I start to make a game plan of how we're going to approach this going forward.

Now, I frequently find a huge mistake that a lot of clients make when dealing with a tax professional who does not know how to handle resolution cases. They'll just rush into filing tax returns. They haven't filed their tax returns in years, and all of a sudden they'll file 13 years' worth of tax returns!

TMI!

There's no reason to break the law of omerta and then spill out everything you can think of! A little caution, my friend. A good friend of mine who is a criminal tax attorney tells people to think before they file!

The IRS manual says we only have to file the past six years to be considered compliant. That is the legal requirement. Well, if you have tax returns that were due 10 years ago and you have a big liability, if you haven't filed, and the IRS hasn't come after you, it's because the IRS has issued what's called a substitute return on your behalf. If I go ahead and file returns, I might create a $15,000, $20,000 or who-knows-what massive liability that didn't need to go on your record because the IRS already has you down for a certain amount. We don't want to mess with that. That's why a game plan is really important.

Now here's the thing. Even though the IRS requires only six years of returns for you to be considered compliant, your state, especially the state of California, requires that all your tax returns must be filed no matter what. So, if you have an tax return missing from 15 years ago and they know it's missing, that return has to be filed. No ifs, ands, or buts about it. We've got to file the return, and to file that state return, we've got to file the federal return to be able to create that state return. So that is part of the game plan: coordinating the filing of state and federal returns for your best outcome.

Now another part of this game plan is that we've got to make sure we do it correctly. With my California clients, if there are state liabilities, I'm filing those state tax returns before I file the federal tax returns.

There's a reason behind that. The state of California is going to want their money. They're 1,000 times more aggressive, I believe, than the IRS, and we want to get that resolution with them as soon as possible. The IRS will allow us to use our payment arrangement or our resolution options with the state as a consideration when we are coming up with the IRS solution.

There's a game plan behind getting caught up on your taxes and becoming compliant. These are the things that we have to do to move forward into the next phase of becoming compliant.

To wrap this up, again, we got to do that investigation of liability, we've got to have a really good interview process to find out everything that happened. I've got to pull the transcripts. I always pull 10 years' worth of transcripts. I'm going back 10 years to see what's happened in the last 10 years; that way we don't miss anything. If we need to do a Freedom of Information Act to get the IRS's notes on a certain case file, we will do that as well. Then once I have that information, we make our game plan to move forward into the next phase, and that next phase is going to be the compliance part.

STEP 2

I can't help you make the IRS an offer they can't refuse until something very significant happens. That something is "compliance." Compliance means you are up to date with filing your tax returns and paying what you owe this quarter. Just this quarter, for now.

When you're trying to resolve tax matters with the IRS, you have a number of different options, but none of them will be possible until you are in compliance.

I know, I know. It's a hassle! But it is a necessary step toward getting you any leverage with the IRS so you can settle the headache your taxes have become. Once you are in compliance, they understand that you are cooperating, and they will work with you.

What does compliance mean? It does not mean handing over tens of thousands of back taxes yesterday, although that is an option and a good one, if you've got the money. In fact, if you've got the money to do it, paying everything you owe ASAP is your best possible tax resolution strategy.

But that's not necessary to be in compliance.

Compliance means that your unfiled tax returns from the past get done and filed. Sorry. That's just the way it is. The IRS won't be interested in making a workable plan with you unless you are in compliance.

The second part of compliance is paying your current taxes. That can mean only paying the taxes you estimate you owe for this quarter of the year, which is three months. That's not so scary, right?

Once you take those two steps, you can start breathing easier, because the solution to your problems is launched. You are beginning already to enter into a more positive relationship with the IRS. You have shown your good will, and they will respond.

We have to do the complete financials and mail it in to the IRS. It is very similar to applying for mortgage. The IRS wants to know everything about your finances, to determine what type of plan you qualify for. We'll make a request for an installment or other type of plan later. We may even find that you don't owe all the taxes you think you do. But we can't make an offer they can't refuse yet until we get you in compliance first.

Now, at some point, either you or I are going to call the IRS and talk to them. I know that most people would like to avoid that the way Bonasera wanted to avoid being in debt to the Godfather, but it's part of the deal. A phone call promising to get into compliance, submit financials, and propose a resolution will get you a thirty delay, very politely given, right away.

Always be polite and professional if you talk to the IRS. It pays.

You could do this yourself, but I know it's scary to do that, so as your godfather, I will do it for you. Bingo! The big bad wolf of the IRS has been contacted, is no longer growling with his teeth dripping as he salivates for your blood, and you are on your way to having a clear conscience about coming a little closer to being in good standing with this powerful agency.

STEP 3

So, let's talk about the final step, tax resolution. Now, throughout this book, I talk about a variety of different items that we can do to resolve tax debt. The next chapter goes into ten such options.

Ultimately, though, the game plan for tax resolution usually comes down to three broad areas. It's a lot more detailed than what I am going to discuss here, but I just want to give you a broad overview.

The first resolution is what's called a CNC, which means Currently Not Collectible. That basically means that you are unable to pay off the debt that you currently have, based on your current income and the expenses that the IRS deems allowable. So part of this step is us doing a complete financial overview to see what your current income is and what your current allowable expenses are.

Believe it or not, the IRS has specific guidelines on what you're allowed to spend on housing, food, and transportation. There are quite a few items that they will allow. Based on that, the IRS looks at the money that's left over that shows whether you have the ability to make good on your past-due tax debt. If you don't have anything left over, you can't pay your tax debt, and it is currently not collectible (CNC).

Option two is an installment agreement. There are actually six different versions of installment agreements. I'm not going to dive deep into all of them. I'll give you a sampling. What the installment agreement basically says is that, based on the amount of debt that you currently owe, and the amount of money that is available to be used towards your tax debt, you have the ability to make payments to the IRS. You may have the ability to pay off the entire tax debt within the statute of limitations or you may be able to pay off a portion of the debt within that time frame.

That's called a partial paid installment agreement. Let's say you owe $90,000, but there's no way you're going to be able to pay that off within the statute of limitations that the IRS allows. But there is leftover money to pay, so the IRS will basically say, "Well, you're going to pay X amount of dollars over the next five years." That amount might be $20,000 that you pay off in the timeframe that they're allowing. So you basically just got away with what's called a partial-pay installment agreement. It can be a very good deal. In this example, the person only paid about 25% of the debt.

The next major tax resolution strategy is what we typically hear on the radio or on late-night television. It's called the OIC or the Offer in Compromise. Basically, you ask the IRS, based on your current financial situation and the amount of debt that you owe, if they will accept a certain amount of money to cover the past-due tax liability and call it even.

Let's say you owe several hundred thousand dollars. You owe that amount of money, but based on your financial situation, there's no way you're going to be able to pay that off within the statute of limitation. Say you offer them $3,000 you have in an IRA in lieu of the hundreds of thousands. The IRS will approve that if that is the best that they can get. That could be a massive blessing in disguise.

This option, though, as great as it sounds, is also one of the toughest for you to keep your promise on, and here's why. With an offer in compromise, you promise you cannot get yourself into tax problems for the next five years. You have to file all your tax returns on time. In the year with any tax liability, you have to keep your nose clean, because if you fail to follow their guidelines, they will come back and reissue the entire debt. It is a great option if you qualify for it and you kind of stick to your guns and make sure you don't get yourself in trouble.

The IRS approves very few OICs. It does happen, though. I think the reason the approval rate is so low is that there are too many tax practitioners and tax mills. They submit an offer in compromise for everyone who steps into their offices, knowing that they don't qualify, and then they get denied.

Wesley Snipes is a recent example of a tax case where someone tried to do an offer in compromise. He owed millions upon millions of dollars. He offered dramatically less than that. Just by looking at the overview of the case, I could have told you, as could probably any professional tax resolution expert that handles these types of cases, the IRS was not going to accept that offer. This individual had huge ability to continue making money. The IRS wanted a bigger chunk of change, and they were right.

Sometimes I think my main job as a tax consultant is just to open your eyes to all the possibilities that are available. There are even more options waiting in the next chapter.

Chapter 3

TAX RESOLUTION OPTIONS

Now there are ten "Big Options" to getting things square with the IRS. These are your Tax Resolution Options, so let's take a quick look at each one.

BIG OPTION 1 – FULL PAY THE TAX OWED

While seldom a popular option, this option changes things fast! Honestly, it is the simplest way to go, if you can do it. That is why it is Big Option Number 1: it really is the best.

I just had a prospect recently came in. She had $30,000 worth of tax debt; she was getting sick with the stress of dealing with the tax debt; she was getting letters from the IRS; she wasn't sleeping, pacing the floor all night--all the challenges that people go through when they have tax problems. As I was doing the initial interview, I had asked her, "In regards to finances, are you currently working?" She was like, "No." So I'm thinking, "Well, you know what? This might be a Currently Not Collectible candidate. She can't afford to pay for it on a monthly basis. She's not working."

Then I asked a simple question, "Do you have any type of savings or retirement accounts?" She said, "Yeah, I've got close to half a million dollars in my retirement account."

I was dumbstruck. I was thinking, "Wait a second. You have a half a million dollars in your retirement account, but you're stressing out and getting sick over a $30,000 debt with the IRS?" So I asked her, "Why not just pull the money out, pay off the IRS, and be done with it?"

Her big thing was that she didn't want to get a penalty for taking money out of her retirement account. Well, there are penalties and interest being added on to overdue taxes every day.

It's hard for me to sit here and try to even write about this, because it was a simple problem to fix. When I walked her through how simple this was to fix, literally the next day, she actually called me and said her tax problems had been taken care of. She called the retirement company, pulled the money out, and paid it directly to the IRS.

Done. Tax problem gone.

Pay your full amount owed, and the IRS will fall silent. You will enjoy a blessed peace. It's worth it if you've got the money, trust me.

Most people don't have the money to pay their tax debt in full right up front, though. That's why there are other options.

BIG OPTION 2 – FILING UNFILED TAX RETURNS AND REPLACING SUBSTITUTE FOR RETURNS

When resolving a tax problem, it is relatively common to have unfiled back tax returns. But guess what? That doesn't mean you aren't on record with the IRS as owing for those years.

When the IRS notices that you haven't filed a tax return for the last few years, they are nice enough to do it for you! Yep! This is called a "Substitute for a Return." They figure out what you may owe if there are forms on file with them like W-2 and 1099 forms relating to you. Guess what? The IRS considers that you owe them the money they figured you did, and they can also move to enforce or collect.

So getting in there and filing the tax returns you didn't file and replacing Substitute for Returns with real returns is a tax resolution option.

BIG OPTION 3 – DISPUTE THE TAX ON TECHNICAL GROUNDS

If there is a technical basis to dispute the amount of tax owed, we might be able to get the IRS to back off by telling them we have some doubts as to your actual liability. This doesn't involve any financial analysis about whether you can pay it or not; you are just trying to show that you really shouldn't have to pay it because you don't owe it. We call it filing a "Doubt as to Liability" form.

It would be nice if the IRS would just take your word or my word for it that you don't owe this because of blah-blah-blah, but in fact you are going to have to provide documentation that shows you really don't owe this money.

Good luck to you, my friend. If you legitimately owe the IRS money, even the godfather can't help you here.

BIG OPTION 4 – CURRENTLY NOT COLLECTIBLE STATUS

We've already covered this in the previous chapter: CNC. You simply don't have the ability to make any monthly payments to pay down your tax debt. You just ain't got it. You are going to have to submit financial information to prove that. You are going to have to show that your income is taken up by your expenses (the allowable ones) and that you don't have any assets that can be sold for money to pay the tax bill. You do this by filing a Collection Information Statement 433 for your personal finances, your self-employment and/or wage-earner status, or your business if you own one (forms 433-F, 43e3-A, 433-B, respectively). Beware: The IRS would love for you to fill out these forms yourself. I would never allow my client to fill out these forms without first reviewing every line item on this form to make sure you can get the best possible outcome.

If you have the documentation right on this, the government will code your tax bill as being uncollectible. You'll still owe it, but they won't do anything to collect it.

What's more, the ten-year statute of limitations clock will start, and you may be able to wait it out if your financials stay the same. After a ten-year window, the IRS has to stop all attempts to collect.

BIG OPTION 5 – INSTALLMENT AGREEMENTS

I've covered this, in the previous chapter, but here are a few more details. In general, the IRS will go for things like:

A Streamlined Agreement: If you owe less than $100,000 and can pay in full over 84 months, you can get one of these going with a phone call or through the website IRS.gov. Very easy. One and done.

A Regular Agreement - if you can't pay back over 84 months, you send in a 433A - Collection Information Statement. The government then sets up for you a monthly installment plan.

In both of the above agreements, if you keep paying your installments and stay in compliance with your taxes, you can relax. The IRS will leave you happily alone.

You could also do a **Partial-Pay Agreement**, as I noted before. This is pretty much the same, except every 12 to 18 months, they will revisit your agreement, and they will want new financials from you to see if you can pay more.

BIG OPTION 6 – THE OFFER IN COMPROMISE

We've covered the IRS Offer in Compromise program. As your godfather, if this is our best bet, I will make sure we use this option to the fullest capacity. I will help you make an offer to the IRS that they can't refuse!

BIG OPTION 7 – PENALTY ABATEMENTS

Unfortunately, you may owe more than back taxes. The IRS can stick you with penalties and fines too. If you have only missed filing for one year, you might be able to get that penalty waived if you can prove that a big, unusual event prevented you from filing and paying your taxes, as I mentioned before. It has to be significant, though, like a death in the family, an illness or injury that took you out of commission, being unemployed or downsized, being put in prison, or certain natural disasters and their effects.

BIG OPTION 8 – DISCHARGING TAXES IN BANKRUPTCY

Most of the time tax liabilities aren't included in bankruptcies, but they can be. You can't discharge Substitute for Returns, though (another good reason to get into compliance). Yet income tax forms that were filed voluntarily without fraud, and within three years of when it was due, may be eligible.

If you are declaring bankruptcy, make sure your bankruptcy lawyer understands tax law. That kind of person may be hard to find, but he or she can possibly get some of your tax debt discharged in bankruptcy, and that is worth doing.

BIG OPTION 9 – INNOCENT SPOUSE RELIEF

It is not uncommon to find yourself in trouble with the IRS because of your spouse or ex-spouse's actions. In most couples, one of the people handles the details of the finances and the other just goes along. It is possible to prove that you, as an innocent spouse, really have no tax liability for some of the shenanigans your spouse pulled off. This is an option for the non-financial partner in the marriage who really had nothing to do with the tax mess they are both in.

BIG OPTION 10 - EXPIRATION OF THE COLLECTION STATUTE

Now, the IRS only has a limited time during which to collect back taxes from you. Basically, it is ten years. Your tax liabilities have a Collection Statute Expiration Date (CSED).

The ten years begin to run on the date of the particular tax assessment. This assessment usually comes in the form of a bill from the IRS.

If you haven't filed in, like, forever, some of your tax liabilities may have timed out. Wonderful! Sometimes all things come to he or she who waits! That doesn't mean I'm recommending omerta, but there is only so long the IRS can try to collar you for back taxes. The statute of limitations is ten years.

Now you know that you have ten big options that may be used to offset the taxes you owe. You do have options. This will not be a slam dunk for the IRS. All you need is a godfather to figure out which one or combination will work best for you.

Chapter 4

DETERMINING WHEN YOU NEED PROFESSIONAL ASSISTANCE

You always have the option of representing yourself. I can't honestly say I recommend this.

REPRESENTING YOURSELF BEFORE THE IRS

For one thing, people like me speak the IRS's language. We know what they want. We know what they need. We know what they will respond to and what they won't respond to.

Also, we are less emotionally involved than you are. We care what happens to you, yes. But ultimately it is not our problem; it is yours. So when we pore over your documents or your financials, we just see the facts, figures, and options. We want to get the best deal for you, but we don't get a shot of adrenaline coursing through our veins every time we hear "IRS." We're used to it all. We know how routine and common most of this is!

Also, because we're pros, we can save you money! That's how your godfather looks out for you!

The single greatest advantage of representing yourself in front of the IRS is that it won't cost you any professional fees.

Again, it might be tempting to represent yourself. But I firmly believe that you will not lose by paying the fee of a tax professional. I think you will recoup that fee, probably several times over.

Tax Professionals to Consider

If someone is an Enrolled Agent, like I am, they have the highest credentials the IRS is going to give someone. Not meaning to brag, but it's true. So using an EA is a good way to go.

Enrolled Agents are actually authorized by the IRS to represent taxpayers. They pass a stringent test, or else they have worked for the IRS for a minimum of five years. Plus, they have to update their knowledge every three years by taking 72 hours of continuing education. They are federally-licensed, and the IRS recognizes them as expert representatives. They're also background-checked like crazy by the IRS. They are tax experts second to none.

Don't go to a tax preparer. Some of them have to look up the rules as they do your taxes! I've seen this! Some of them are less informed than their clients.

EAs and some certified public accountants (CPAs) and tax lawyers know the tax code in and out, and they keep up with every small change too. They are your best bet when looking for a tax consulting firm. Make sure there are people like the above in it.

Make sure one of them is at your service. Another thing to check is: does this particular EA, CPA, or lawyer deal with situations like yours? Is your tax situation personal? Does it relate to your small business? Your large business? It all makes a difference.

HOW TO FIND A TAX PROFESSIONAL

If you already have an accountant, attorney, or other professional advisors, that person may be able to recommend a good tax professional.

PERSONAL REFERRALS

Do you have a friend or acquaintance who has gone through tax problems with good results? His or her advisor may be available or be able to refer you to someone who is.

PROFESSIONAL ASSOCIATIONS

The National Association of Enrolled Agents (NAEA) can direct you to an EA who is in your local area. The ABA (American Bar Association) can direct you to attorneys near you too. Your state has a board of accountancy you can refer to in order to find a CPA.

Don't go it alone. If you have tax issues, you need the help of a professional to sort them out.

Tax Resolution Resource

If you need to speak with the "Godfather" go to TaxDebtBook.com to book an appointment or call 909.570.1103

Chapter 5

TIME: IT'S EITHER ON YOUR SIDE OR THE IRS'S

Just about everything the IRS can do to you has a time limit associated with it. The biggest time limit the IRS observes is the ten-year statute of limitations. We've already mentioned this, but let's go into a little more detail.

A statute of limitations means that legal action can only be taken against someone within a certain time frame. If the statute of limitations runs out, even if the person committed some wrongdoing, they can't be prosecuted. It's just too late. This applies to both civil infractions and criminal infractions (however, there is no statute of limitations on the crime of murder).

If you've received a tax assessment that shows you owe, the IRS has a ten-year window to collect those taxes. They can sometimes get around this, but, in general, they will not collect taxes that were assessed more than ten years ago.

That's if you filed! If you haven't filed, their ten-year limit doesn't count, so don't think the head-in-the-sand approach is best for the next decade!

NO OMERTA!

If you're like I was, or if you've been following the law of omerta too diligently and haven't filed for ten years, that doesn't mean you are home free home. Like I said before, the IRS sometimes files on your behalf—one or more of those Substitute for Returns may be lingering in your tax background. What's more, the clock is not running on their ten-year statute of limitations if you never filed.

In general, the IRS has three years back to question (audit) any of your tax returns, and ten years to collect any taxes they say you owe. You also have three years from the date of filing to get any tax refunds you are owed.

Sometimes just filing those missing returns can clear up a lot of problems for you. You may get returns for some years that will help you pay off tax debts from other years.

Again, don't run and hide or observe the law of omerta or silence about any all tax activities. Let's get working on it and get time on your side, not the IRS's.

Chapter 6

NASTY THINGS THE IRS CAN DO TO YOU

The IRS has a lot of power when it comes to enforced collection, which means that they can make you pay, one way or another. The following are their major means of extracting the bucks out of you.

The first is the most common; it goes into the public record, and it can affect your ability to get loans, jobs, and can harm your business's reputation.

FEDERAL TAX LIENS

Once the IRS makes a valid assessment against you, and you have not paid the debt, they can put a lien on your property. Ouch! That includes real estate (like your house), personal property (like your car, jewelry, valuable furnishings, etc), and any financial assets (like stocks or bonds or other investments). Once they've sent you a Notice and Demand for Payment and you've been following the law of omerta and didn't respond—well, they can come after your stuff.

Now you've got issues.

I told you the law of omerta didn't work here!

You have a few options though.

CERTIFICATE OF DISCHARGE

You can apply for a Certificate of Discharge (COD). You can ask the IRS for one of these if the lien was filed prematurely or improperly; or if you are already in an installment agreement with the IRS; or if withdrawal of the lien will facilitate payment of the tax liability; OR if your Taxpayer Advocate thinks that withdrawal of the lien is in your best interest and in the government's best interest.

That's where a godfather can come in—convincing the IRS of that last point.

LIEN SUBORDINATION

The IRS might agree that their lien on your property can be subordinated or put behind other financial obligations or debts you have. This can lessen the impact of a federal tax lien.

CERTIFICATE OF RELEASE OF PAID OR UNENFORCEABLE LIEN

The IRS is required to issue a certificate of release of lien no later than 30 days after you've paid them what you owe them. They have to let you go! That's why paying in full as fast as possible is always the best option. It's also hard to do for most people.

However, once you've fulfilled your tax obligation, you will get such a certificate of release.

If you haven't paid, but the ten-year statute of limitations has run out on the IRS being able to collect it, or it is unenforceable for some other reason, the IRS must give you a certificate of release.

Phew! It's always good to get one of these--and the IRS doesn't always just hand them out. Usually, you need to get them yourself, with the help of a tax professional.

BANK ACCOUNT LEVIES

An IRS levy is the actual action taken by the IRS to literally take your money out of your pockets. They can legally do this! In their own words (irs.gov) the IRS says that it can levy (that means "take" or "seize"):

"wages, retirement accounts, dividends, bank accounts, licenses, rental income, accounts receivables, the cash loan value of your life insurance, or commissions)."

PERSONAL PROPERTY LEVIES

Or, the IRS could, again, in their own words: "seize and sell property that you hold (such as your car, boat or house)."

The IRS's levy power is extremely broad and deep.

SEIZURES

The IRS seizure of homes and business is much rarer than it used to be, but does still happen. They can come and take your stuff.

What is more, they can get to your employer and take part of your wages.

WAGE GARNISHMENTS

The IRS wage garnishment is when they send a letter to your employer (Publication 1494) and explain that they want a portion of your wages. They look at how many dependents you have and your general status. Generally, they won't take all of your wages, but if you have other sources of income, they can!

FAIR DEBT COLLECTION PRACTICES ACT

The IRS is subject to the conditions of the Fair Debt Collection Practices Act just like any other debt collector. But here's where it can get a little scary. The IRS is now hiring private debt collectors to get taxpayers' owed money. Some of these people make phone calls--lots of them! Yet one of the most famous scams is someone calling you and telling you that you owe taxes to the IRS and need to hand over your credit card number right now! What's a person to do?

First off, you will still get letters in the mail from the IRS before any phone calls start. That way you will know whether these people are scamming you or really represent your IRS tax debt. Also, they will direct you to electronic payment at the IRS website. They won't take credit card payments or such over the phone.

If you are in it deep and have been for years, it is possible they will turn your account over to a collection agency. Still, they can't call you before 8:00 a.m. or after 9:00 p.m. They can't tell you that the sheriff is coming to arrest you. They can't harass or hassle you. Still, they are likely to be at least somewhat of a pain.

Hey, have them call your Enrolled Agent. The godfather will work to get them off your case.

Tax Resolution Resource

If you need to speak with the "Godfather" go to TaxDebtBook.com to book an appointment or call 909.570.1103

Chapter 7

MINIMIZING YOUR TAX BILL: IT ALL STARTS WITH YOUR TAX RETURNS

No more omerta on filing your tax returns! Silence won't buy you peace in this case. What's more, your tax returns are your best possible way to minimize your tax bill and maximize your returns.

Publication 17 from the IRS is your guide to file a tax return. Now, you might see all kinds of books or ebooks on offer out there that promise you the moon when it comes to reducing your taxes. In fact, a lot of these books are just annotated versions of Pub 17, which you can read for yourself.

You can get it here: https://www.irs.gov/pub/irs-pdf/p17.pdf. You can get it in pdf, html, or you can get an ebook.

It isn't a bad idea to familiarize yourself with Pub 17. Knowledge is power, after all. It tells you a lot about how to do everything.

There's a general overview of a tax return, including information on filing, filing status, dependents, tax withholding, and estimated tax.

Then it goes into various categories, like the following:

INCOME

The guide shows you how to account for your income, including wages, tips, interest, dividends, rental income and expenses, retirement plans, pensions, annuities, Social Security, and other sources of income.

The IRS wants to know how much you make and in what form you make it, from what sources it comes from. Don't observe the law of omerta here. Most income is traceable. Own up to what you make.

ADJUSTMENTS

The IRS is interested in your adjusted gross income; they allow you to subtract certain things from your income. These include contributions you make to IRAs (both traditional and Roth), alimony, student loan interest, certain business expenses, and other adjustments that they cover in detail.

DEDUCTIONS

You can also claim the Standard Deduction (raised significantly in 2019), portions of medical and dental expenses, some taxes, some interest expenses, some contributions, and some losses due to theft and other calamities. There is a list of other deductions you can take, and you can also deduct qualified business expenses.

Bottom line: Don't be shy, claim EVERY tax benefit you're legally entitled to! Let an Enrolled Agent work on it with you, because the laws change and new deductions or little known ones can sometimes be found that you would not find yourself.

Don't observe the law of omerta here! Claim everything you can, as long as it is allowed legally and you provide accurate figures. This will directly affect how much you owe.

EXEMPTIONS

There are exemptions (credits) allowed too. If you have dependent children, education credits, Earned Income Credits, and others, these can be subtracted from your income to give you your final, taxable income. If you are over 65, you can claim an elderly credit as well. Once again, a tax professional can help you navigate these available credits to help you take all the ones to which you are entitled.

Important: Exemptions apply to those non-filers-but only through 2017, from 2018-2025- we have tax credits instead of exemptions.

TAXABLE INCOME AND TAX

You can then consult the Tax Table and see what percentage you must pay from your adjusted income. Again, this changes from time to time, so it is important to work with someone who is abreast of tax laws or get the most updated tables.

OTHER TAXES

Your state tax debt comes into consideration as well. It can be deducted from the federal taxes you will owe. Although it has now been repealed and will not figure in 2019 taxes, the health care tax, known as the individual mandate, must be paid as a tax. If you don't have employee health care or have not purchased insurance, this amount will be added to the taxes you owe for the years it has been in force.

TAX CREDITS

See above under "Exemptions."

REFUND OR AMOUNT YOU OWE

After a whirligig of subtractions and percentages, your tax professional will come up with a bottom line figure. If it is less than zero, the IRS owes you. Anything over zero, you owe the IRS.

Most likely, a tax professional will help you do your taxes in such a way as to maximize your return and minimize what you owe.

When it comes to taxes, you want all the breaks that you can legally get! EAs know tax law in and out, and they know what is allowed. Go for all that the law will allow, but let a tax professional guide you so you know exactly what that is.

Tax Resolution Resource

For additional, up to date tips for
minimizing your tax bill and maximizing
refunds on your tax returns, please visit
TaxDebtConsultant.com

Chapter 8

UNDERSTANDING IRS COLLECTIONS AND THE RESOLUTION PROCESS

The U.S. Internal Revenue Service is the single largest collections agency in the country. Congress has given the IRS immense collection power.

COLLECTIONS STARTS WITH A TAX DEFICIENCY

The IRS sends you a bill if you haven't paid the taxes you owe for a given year. That comes in the form of a letter, and it will include penalties and interest from the date of the time the debt was assessed.

The interest compounds daily, and a late penalty is charged monthly. It can really add up.

If you don't pay the first bill you receive, you'll get a second one and maybe one or two more.

NO OMERTA!

Trying to hide from these bills and shoving them under your mattress and zipping your lip about them will not save you from the IRS! Open them up and see what they say and form an action plan to start taking care of the debt. If you don't act fast, the IRS will start collection activities against you; meanwhile, the penalties and monthly late fees just keep adding up.

Contact them. You can put any of the ten options in place that I talked about in Chapter 2: all your possible options. Get a godfather, though, to help you.

The last thing you want to do is observe the law of omerta. It will work against you with the IRS.

NOTICE OF FEDERAL TAX LIEN FILING (FORM 668-Y)

If you fail to pay your tax bill, the IRS can start all those unsettling liens we talked about in Chapter 5. You do not want this to happen. This goes on the public record, and people will not want to loan you money or extend you credit if they know the IRS is after you. They may not want to rent you an apartment or home.

You will receive a Notice of Federal Tax Lien Filing (Form 668-Y),

Don't hide from it. Even the IRS tells you to contact a godfather (a tax professional) when this baby shows up in the mail.

NOTICE OF INTENT TO LEVY (FORM LETTER CP-504)

Once again, if you don't pay your taxes or else you fail to contact the IRS and make a plan with them to pay (you are following the law of omerta), they will send you a Notice of Intent to Levy (Form Letter CP-504). That means they can take your property and sell it. Yes, forget the yard sale or the car ad on craigslist. The IRS will do the selling for you, and they won't give you any of the profits!

Usually they will send you a Final Notice of Intent to Levy and Notice of Your Right to a Hearing at least 30 days before the seizure (see the next section) before they levy (seize) any property.

Now, they can't take everything and leave you out in the street. They can't take your unemployment benefits if you are receiving them. Some pensions and annuities are exempt, worker's com., service-connected disability payments, public assistance or a minimum weekly amount of income. They're not going to take your clothes. They don't always take your house or business assets.

FINAL NOTICE OF INTENT TO LEVY (LETTER 1058)

Exactly 30 days after a CP-504 is issued, you're going to receive your Final Notice of Intent to Levy (Letter 1058).

I really hope you don't leave this one unopened and unanswered because this means they can start making their moves on you.

THE CYCLE REPEATS

They'll send you plenty of notices. You will get a CP14, CP501, CP503, and then that nasty CP504. Up until that time, you have basically been put on notice and send a couple of reminders. It all takes some time, but the process won't go away. To think it will is wishful thinking.

REVENUE OFFICER ASSIGNMENT

Your first time through this cycle, the IRS is still fairly benign. When they assign you a revenue officer, they are getting serious, and, if you haven't done so before now, you'd best get serious at this time.

This is the person who puts the levies into place. This is a person assigned specifically to your case.

Now, most tax debt cases are handled automatically through the Automated Collections System. This generates all those routine, form letters you have been getting. If you owe a lot of taxes, though--say, over $100,000--or your case is really messed up, they're going to give you a person.

This person is not an auditor (sigh of relief). He or she is a collector of monies--your monies. The person can't arrest you (sigh of relief). He or she is supposed to get in touch with you personally, which means he or she will likely come to your door. Anyone telephoning you and posing as an RO probably isn't one. Scam time. Observe the law of omerta, and don't tell a phone caller anything!

Do not observe the law of omerta with your RO, though. This person can't take your house or your car, but he or she can levy your accounts and get a lot of your money. What's more, this person is authorized and trained to get all the financial information out of you he or she can.

The RO can legally come to your house or your place of business. This in and of itself is scary. Plus, they aren't who they are because they aren't smart and tough.

Don't face an RO alone. This is when you really need a godfather on your side.

THE TAX RESOLUTION PROCESS

Whether your case is still assigned to ACS, or if it's been assigned to a Revenue Officer, there is still a fairly standard, step-by-step process by which your tax case gets resolved. A tax professional such as an EA can walk you through it and walk by your side throughout it.

All is not lost, even if the IRS has sent an RO out after you. A godfather can offer you all the protections to which you are legally entitled.

Chapter 9

FILING UNFILED TAX RETURNS AND REPLACING SUBSTITUTE FOR RETURNS

As mentioned in a previous chapter, a Substitute for Return (SFR) is a tax return prepared by the IRS based on what information they have on you in a given year. As I said, when the IRS sits up and notices that you haven't filed a tax return for the last few years, they care about you so much, they file your returns for you! Aren't they sweet? They also figure you owe the taxes stated on any SFR, whether you are aware of its existence or not. What's more, the IRS can move to collect on this tax debt. Not so sweet.

You would know all about this, but you've been observing the law of omerta about any and all tax matters, as well as subjecting all correspondence from the IRS to the same law of omerta and not opening any of it. In fact, the IRS has sent you notice of every SFR they filed on your behalf and how much tax debt you owe on them. Yep! Big Brother knows, even if you don't know they know!

The IRS bases Substitute for Returns on income you have received that has been reported to them from various sources: W-2s from an employer who reports what tax was withheld on your wages, or 1099s that employers or clients or anyone who has paid you money have reported on *their* tax returns. The IRS cooks up a Substitute for Return based on the financial information they have about you on record that can give them an idea of what you owe.

Getting rid of these Substitutes for Returns by replacing them with real returns can wind up helping you financially. It is very often the case that filing your own tax return will benefit you more as far as tax debt goes than the IRS substitute. That's because the IRS doesn't do any deductions for you, and it doesn't give you any tax credits. Heck, they might even owe you, but their Substitute for Return shows you in the red. You might end up getting some tax refunds you didn't know you were owed if you file your own original tax return, and this can help reduce the tax debt you have.

Also, as mentioned before, you might be able to discharge some tax debts through bankruptcy. You can't discharge Substitutes for Returns, though.

Caution, caution, caution, though! Do not merrily file every tax return you or your tax preparer can think of!

OMERTA! This is the one place where it applies! Don't spill your guts here! Legally, you only have to file for the past six years to be compliant. If you are going to go back to the Roosevelt Administration, you might end up owing a massive amount of tax debt!

What's more, the ten-year statute of limitations started running on those Substitute for Returns, even if you never signed them. You might have run out the clock on some of your tax debt.

So don't get so over-eager about cleaning up your past that you do more than you have to do. Not wise. Let's look at those Substitute for Returns and see if replacing them with original tax returns will benefit you. Let's not throw any advantages away. We want you to be in compliance, not in cahoots with creating your own financial doom.

Please do get a pro on your side in this. Tax preparers--well, some of them only work during the peak of the tax season, and then they go back to their regular jobs as plumbers, ditch diggers, real estate agents, and doting aunts. Of course, I recommend getting an EA, Enrolled Agent, because our kind understands all the ins and outs and will find you the best, safest, most economical route to resolve all those old issues without jumping overboard and paying more than you legally owe.

An EA like me will get power of attorney from you, and I will have the ability to get every ounce of information the IRS has about you. I can file a Freedom of Information Act request to get the notes of any auditors who came sniffing around your finances. This kind of information--knowledge--is power. We will know exactly where you are at with the IRS, and that means we will know exactly where you need to go to get clean and straight with them again without unnecessarily harming yourself.

Get the best help you can. The next chapter will show you how.

Tax Resolution Resource

For assistance in preparing your overdue tax returns and replacing Substitute for Returns, please visit TaxDebtConsultant.com

Chapter 10

FIVE QUESTIONS TO ASK ANY TAX RESOLUTION FIRM BEFORE SHELLING OUT A DIME

I think I've made it clear that when resolving a longstanding case of omerta about your tax returns, it is best to consult a godfather– a professional tax resolution consultant, preferably an EA. He or she can save you much grief and financial pain. Resolving your tax liabilities is important enough to conduct research on the tax resolution firm(s) you are considering before agreeing to purchase their services.

Don't choose the wrong godfather! It's the difference between choosing Don Corleone and Virgil Sollozzo. At least Don Corleone behaved according to a system of Mafia and Sicilian honor and justice. He had some scruples. For Virgil Sollozzo, on the other hand, anyone and anything was fair game. He'd stop at nothing–even introducing narcotics into general society–to make the big bucks. (For the record, Michael Corleone whacked Sollozzo in an Italian restaurant for trying to murder his father, the godfather.)

I'm not saying other tax professionals are unscrupulous. Some are; some aren't. They may be inexperienced, though. They may not know when to quit. Their credentials might be on the shady side. They may not be as wise as you hope they are.

Here are five questions that will help you conduct your "due diligence" in selecting a tax professional or godfather to get you out of your taxation woes.

QUESTION #1: ARE YOU LICENSED TO BE PROVIDING ME TAX ADVICE?

Many tax resolution firms use unlicensed sales personnel to sell their services.

These salespeople do not possess the professional knowledge to be advising you on your tax matters, nor are they legally allowed to do so.

The only people that can advise you on tax matters are Enrolled Agents (EAs), Certified Public Accountants (CPAs), and attorneys. Ask the person you're speaking to whether they are licensed. If they say anything other than EA, CPA, or attorney, then they are not licensed.

Some salespeople have even been known to make up something or just give you their title at their firm ("Senior Tax Analyst," for example). Several people have received criminal convictions for this kind of misrepresentation, but it still occurs.

QUESTION #2: CAN I MEET YOU IN PERSON?

Ask the company if you can meet them in person at their local office to discuss your tax situation. Most companies that advertise on radio, TV, or even on the Internet will never give you the option to meet in person! That should be a big red flag. If they can't afford or don't have a brick-and-mortar where they can meet clients in person, they are probably not legit.

I am in the City of Redlands and have a local office where I meet with clients every day. We are located at 1255 W. Colton Ave #535, Redlands, CA 92374.

We are directly behind Arby's/Bakers Restaurant in the red-colored executive offices building.

If distance is a problem, I would be happy to set up a Skype, Facebook, or any other Internet meeting so we can look each other eye-to-eye and discuss your tax problem

QUESTION #3: ARE YOU THE ACTUAL PERSON THAT WILL BE REPRESENTING ME?

Before signing a contract for taxpayer representation, be sure to confirm that the firm that will assign your case to a licensed representative.

You should be guaranteed that your representative is a licensed EA, CPA, or attorney, even if it's somebody else in the firm other than the licensed person you're already speaking to. The IRS will not allow non-licensed representatives to negotiate for a taxpayer, but you would be surprised at how often large firms have unlicensed assistants doing the actual IRS negotiations. Not a good idea!

Before you sign a contract or send money, make sure you see the IRS Form 2848, Power of Attorney, which lists the name(s) of the people representing you.

QUESTION #4: HAVE YOU EVER ACTUALLY BEEN INVOLVED IN NEGOTIATING TAX RESOLUTIONS?

In other words, has the person you are speaking to actually worked on tax cases as a representative?

It's one thing to be licensed; it's quite another to have actual case experience or not. Because the government is cracking down on sales practices, some sales closers have taken the Enrolled Agent exam and become licensed.

This is better than not being licensed, of course, but it still does not make them qualified to offer tax advice regarding your IRS debt if they have no actual case experience.

Any case-experienced, licensed salesperson should be able to walk you through the case proceedings from start to finish.

I am not only an Enrolled Agent, licensed by the Department of the Treasury. I also have an NTPI Fellow®. This designation is evidence of significant expertise in the representation of taxpayers before the IRS.

NTPI Fellows have completed a stringent, three-level program of study that covers all facets of representing clients before the IRS. They have learned to guide their clients through the often-challenging maze of IRS codes, internal regulations, and agency structure.

The process of becoming an NTPI Fellow often takes several years, but the learning doesn't stop there.

As a whole, NTPI Fellows are individuals who exceed the IRS's minimum standard for continuing education and are dedicated to staying on top of the latest changes to the tax code.

Get someone who is both qualified and experienced in negotiating tax resolutions. Why should you settle for less?

QUESTION #5: WHAT PRECISELY DOES THE FEE YOU ARE QUOTING ME INCLUDE?

The tax resolution business is notorious for "rebilling" clients for work that either doesn't need to be done, was excessively overbilled for in the first place, or that should have been included in your original fee quote.

Many tax resolution firms operate on a "flat fee" basis. In theory, the fee they quote you should include EVERYTHING necessary to resolve your case.

Make sure that fee includes some of these necessary actions:

- All Appeals files

- Full negotiation of resolution

- Preparation of any missing tax returns

- Removal of any existing levies or wage garnishments

- Representation for all tax types, including state taxes if needed

- For business owners, make sure you are covered for Trust Fund Recovery Penalty representation. This is critical to prevent getting personally stuck with your business tax bill.

- Application for a penalty abatement if you meet "reasonable cause criteria."

If the tax firm you are speaking to works on a retainer basis with hourly fees rather than a flat fee, be sure to see a schedule of service fees, and get a copy of their billing policy. Ask for an estimate of what the total charges will be and get that in writing.

Also, understand that hiring a representative to negotiate on your behalf is not a guarantee that your case will be resolved.

You will need to work closely with your representative to ensure that your best interests are always put front and center. Although your representative should do nearly all the interaction with the taxing authorities, your participation with your representative is vital to the resolution process. Be sure you select somebody that you are going to be able to work with, without personality conflicts.

Lastly, be sure that anything and everything you discuss with a tax resolution firm, such as fees, covered services, responsibilities, deadlines, etc., are all in WRITING.

Don't sign a contract, and definitely don't give them your credit card number without seeing everything in writing first.

QUESTION #5: WHAT IS MY RESPONSIBILITY IN THIS PROCESS?

If I don't get you my files, documents and my materials, will I be

my own worst enemy? Will I be eating up my fee and forcing you to charge me more? Or will you just leave me in the lurch waiting for me to get my paperwork to you? You are the most important person in dealing with the IRS. We guide you through the maze and know your rights, but if you are not working with us nothing gets solved.

It is very similar to joining a gym you can join the gym but if you don't show up nothing happens, and you have just wasted your money.

Armed with these tips, you should be better positioned to make a wise decision regarding hiring professional tax services. Get yourself a good godfather, and your tax woes will clear up, a weight will be lifted from your mind, heart, and shoulders, and you will face the world as a responsible, mature citizen in good standing. It's worth it, believe me.

Now it's time to get help!

In the next chapter, you will learn how to make the most out of your free tax debt analysis for all readers of this book.

Chapter 11

HOW TO GET THE MOST OUT OF YOUR NO-COST TAX DEBT ANALYSIS!

If you've read this book all the way through, you know now the value of moving forward and solving your tax debt problem!

No more "Omerta!"

I am offering all readers of my book a Tax Debt Analysis at no cost! Normally this would cost $300, but for you, no-cost! You are getting 30 minutes of time to see what tax problems you are dealing with and what is the best way to getting "right" with the IRS or state.

All you have to do is mention you read about this offer in my book.

I want you to get the most out of our time together. So, please make sure you first go to MeetWithGodfather.com and book an appointment!

If you need a "virtual appointment" because you are not local, just let me know when you book your appointment, and I will set that up to meet virtually using: Facebook Messenger, Skype, or another online platform.

Here's how to get the most out of our time together:

1. Be prepared with questions. As you're reading through the book, keep a list of things you wish to ask.

2. Prepare all the IRS and state notices you may have opened or left unopened. Bring them in, and we will open them together. There are some important dates in those notices that protect your rights!

3. Download my Case Review worksheet, and fill out as much as possible at
http://taxdebtconsultant.com/casereview/

4. Come ready to have an action plan to keep the IRS/state off your back with me protecting you! Get ready to able to breathe again and sleep all night without waking up. Get ready to answer your phone again, not worried about the IRS calling!

5. I promise you this: you will have an action plan when you leave my office or when we get off the phone.

How to Schedule Your Tax Debt Analysis

Go to MeetWithGodfather.com and book online

Just Call 909.570.1103 – Be prepared to leave a message. The Godfather has a lot of clients daily! But he listens to all his own messages.

ABOUT THE AUTHOR

Juan "Carlos" Samaniego is an entrepreneur, speaker and author. As Enrolled Agent, licensed by the Department of the Treasury and credentialed by the IRS to represent taxpayers on all levels of the administration.

Carlos has the knowledge and expertise to help you reach a favorable outcome with the IRS and State Taxing authorities.

Whether you need assistance with reducing the amount of your tax debt, filing a back-tax return or preparing a tax settlement by negotiating offer-in-compromise, installment agreements, or determining whether you are considered uncollectible. He is ready to help

As an Enrolled Agents he is one of the most knowledgeable tax resolution consultants around. As an Enrolled Agent, he passed rigorous testing, engages in demanding continuing education to keep up with tax code changes, and abides by a code of ethics. He belongs to the National Association of Enrolled Agents.

In addition, Carlos has an NTPI Fellow®. This designation is evidence of significant expertise in the representation of taxpayers before the IRS.

NTPI Fellows have completed a stringent, three-level program of study that covers all facets of representing clients before the IRS.

They have learned to guide their clients through the often-challenging maze of IRS codes, internal regulations, and agency structure.

The process of becoming an NTPI Fellow often takes several years, but the learning doesn't stop there. Rigorous continuing education is stringently required.

As a whole, NTPI Fellows are individuals who exceed the IRS's minimum standard for continuing education and are dedicated to staying on top of the latest changes to the tax code.

The first thing you will notice about Carlos is that he deeply cares about people, he is helping. He grew up the oldest of five, and was raised by parents who believed in the importance of honesty and hard work.

Carlos married his beautiful wife Elizabeth in 2005 who is the co-founder of HealthcareTaxAdvisors LLC and TaxDebtConsultants.

He is also a father too, Andrew, who is midshipman at the United States Navy Academy and will graduate in May 24, 2019 and be commissioned as an officer in the Navy and serve as a Surface Warfare Officer. And he is also the proud dad to his entrepreneurial, Youtuber, daughter Bella who is also the video editor for his company.

He is a member of the National Association of Enrolled Agents, California Society of Enrolled Agents, American Society of Tax Problem Solvers, National Association of Tax Professionals.

Carlos is also in a 18-month study program to become a United States Tax Court Practitioner.

Carlos was the founder and president of Entrepreneur Toastmasters Club in Redlands, California. He has received this Distinguished Toastmaster Award from Toastmasters International.

You can find Carlos at the following

Podcast: TaxDebtConsultants Podcast
Facebook: Facebook.com/TaxDebtConsultants
Facebook.com/CarlosSamaniegoEA
Twitter: @CarlosSamaniego
Linkedin.com/in/carlossamaniego/
Instagram: @jcarlossamaniego
Youtube: Carlos Samaniego EA

Juan Carlos Samaniego, EA, Enrolled Agent - NTPI Fellow®.
Phone: 909-570-1103 Direct Fax: 909-586-9190
Email: Carlos@TaxDebtConsultant.com
Book Appointment: TaxDebtConsultant.com

RESOURCES

Your Rights as a Taxpayer

THE TAXPAYER BILL OF RIGHTS

1. The Right to Be Informed: Taxpayers have the right to know what they need to do to comply with the tax laws. They are entitled to clear explanations of the laws and IRS procedures in all tax forms, instructions, publications, notices, and correspondence. They have the right to be informed of IRS decisions about their tax accounts and to receive clear explanations of the outcomes.

2. The Right to Quality Service: Taxpayers have the right to receive prompt, courteous, and professional assistance in their dealings with the IRS, to be spoken to in a way they can easily understand, to receive clear and easily understandable communications from the IRS, and to speak to a supervisor about inadequate service.

3. The Right to Pay No More than the Correct Amount of Tax: Taxpayers have the right to pay only the amount of tax legally due, including interest and penalties, and to have the IRS apply all tax payments properly.

4. The Right to Challenge the IRS's Position and Be Heard: Taxpayers have the right to raise objections and provide additional documentation in response to formal IRS actions or proposed actions, to expect that the IRS will consider their timely objections and documentation promptly and fairly, and to receive a response if the IRS does not agree with their position.

5. The Right to Appeal an IRS Decision in an Independent Forum: Taxpayers are entitled to a fair and impartial administrative appeal of most IRS decisions, including many penalties, and have the right to receive a written response regarding the Office of Appeals' decision. Taxpayers generally have the right to take their cases to court.

6. The Right to Finality: Taxpayers have the right to know the maximum amount of time they have to challenge the IRS's position as well as the maximum amount of time the IRS has to audit a particular tax year or collect a tax debt. Taxpayers have the right to know when the IRS has finished an audit.

7. The Right to Privacy: Taxpayers have the right to expect that any IRS inquiry, examination, or enforcement action will comply with the law and be no more intrusive than necessary, and will respect all due process rights, including search and seizure protections, and will

provide, where applicable, a collection due process hearing.

8. The Right to Confidentiality: Taxpayers have the right to expect that any information they provide to the IRS will not be disclosed unless authorized by the taxpayer or by law. Taxpayers have the right to expect appropriate action will be taken against employees, return preparers, and others who wrongfully use or disclose taxpayer return information.

9. The Right to Retain Representation: Taxpayers have the right to retain an authorized representative of their choice to represent them in their dealings with the IRS. Taxpayers have the right to seek assistance from a Low Income Taxpayer Clinic if they cannot afford representation.

10. The Right to a Fair and Just Tax System: Taxpayers have the right to expect the tax system to consider facts and circumstances that might affect their underlying liabilities, ability to pay, or ability to provide information timely. Taxpayers have the right to receive assistance from the Taxpayer Advocate Service if they are experiencing financial difficulty or if the IRS has not resolved their tax issues properly and timely through its normal channels.

EXAMINATION, APPEALS, COLLECTIONS, AND REFUNDS

EXAMINATIONS (AUDITS)

We accept most taxpayers' returns as filed. If we inquire about your return or select it for examination, it does not suggest that you are dishonest. The inquiry or examination may or may not result in more tax. We may close your case without change; or, you may receive a refund. The process of selecting a return for examination usually begins in one of two ways. First, we use computer programs to identify returns that may have incorrect amounts. These programs may be based on information returns, such as Forms 1099 and W-2, on studies of past examinations, or on certain issues identied by compliance projects. Second, we use information from outside sources that indicates that a return may have incorrect amounts. These sources may include newspapers, public records, and individuals. If we determine that the information is accurate and reliable, we may use it to select a return for examination. Publication 556, Examination of Returns, Appeal Rights, and Claims for Refund, explains the rules and procedures that we follow in examinations. The following sections give an overview of how we conduct examinations.

BY MAIL

We handle many examinations and inquiries by mail. We will send you a letter with either a request for more information or a reason why we believe a change to your return may be needed. You can respond by mail or you can request a personal interview with an examiner. If you mail us the requested information or provide an explanation, we may or may not agree with you, and we will explain the reasons for any changes. Please do not hesitate to write to us about anything you do not understand.

BY INTERVIEW

If we notify you that we will conduct your examination through a personal interview, or you request such an interview, you have the right to ask that the examination take place at a reasonable time and place that is convenient for both you and the IRS. If our examiner proposes any changes to your return, he or she will explain the reasons for the changes. If you do not agree with these changes, you can meet with the examiner's supervisor.

REPEAT EXAMINATIONS

If we examined your return for the same items in either of the 2 previous years and proposed no change to your tax liability, please contact us as soon as possible so we can see if we should discontinue the examination.

APPEALS

If you do not agree with the examiner's proposed changes, you can appeal them to the Appeals Office of the IRS. Most differences can be settled without expensive and time-consuming court trials.

Your appeal rights are explained in detail in both Publication 5, Your Appeal Rights and How To Prepare a Protest If You Don't Agree, and Publication 556, Examination of Returns, Appeal Rights, and Claims for Refund. If you do not wish to use the Appeals Office or disagree with its findings, you may be able to take your case to the U.S. Tax Court, U.S. Court of Federal Claims, or the U.S. District Court where you live. If you take your case to court, the IRS will have the burden of proving certain facts if you kept adequate records to show your tax liability, cooperated with the IRS, and meet certain other conditions. If the court agrees with you on most issues in your case and finds that our position was largely unjustified, you may be able to recover some of your administrative and litigation costs. You will not be eligible to recover these costs unless you tried to resolve your case administratively, including going through the appeals system, and you gave us the information necessary to resolve the case. Collections Publication 594, The IRS Collection Process, explains your rights and responsibilities regarding payment of federal taxes. It describes: • What to do when you owe taxes. It describes what to do if you get a tax bill and what to do if you think your bill is wrong. It also covers making installment payments, delaying collection action, and submitting an offer in compromise. • IRS collection actions. It covers liens, releasing a lien, levies, releasing a levy, seizures and sales, and release of property. • IRS certification to the State Department of a seriously delinquent tax debt, which will generally result in denial of a passport application and may lead to revocation of a passport. Your collection appeal rights are explained in detail in Publication 1660, Collection Appeal Rights.

INNOCENT SPOUSE RELIEF

Generally, both you and your spouse are each responsible for paying the full amount of tax, interest, and penalties due on your joint return. However, if you qualify for innocent spouse relief, you may be relieved of part or all of the joint liability. To request relief, you must file Form 8857, Request for Innocent Spouse Relief. For more information on innocent spouse relief, see Publication 971, Innocent Spouse Relief, and Form 8857.

POTENTIAL THIRD-PARTY CONTACTS

Generally, the IRS will deal directly with you or your duly authorized representative. However, we sometimes talk with other persons if we need information that you have been unable to provide, or to verify information we have received. If we do contact other persons, such as a neighbor, bank, employer, or employees, we will generally need to tell them limited information, such as your name. The law prohibits us from disclosing any more information than is necessary to obtain or verify the information we are seeking. Our need to contact other persons may continue as long as there is activity in your case. If we do contact other persons, you have a right to request a list of those contacted. Your request can be made by telephone, in writing, or during a personal interview.

Refunds You may file a claim for refund if you think you paid too much tax. You must generally file the claim within 3 years from the date you filed your original return or 2 years from the date you paid the tax, whichever is later. The law generally provides for interest on your refund if it is not paid within 45 days of the date you filed your return or claim for refund. Publication 556, Examination of Returns, Appeal Rights, and Claims for Refund, has more information on refunds. If you were due a refund but you did not file a return, you generally must file your return within 3 years from the date the return was due (including extensions) to get that refund.

TAXPAYER ADVOCATE SERVICE

TAS is an independent organization within the IRS that can help protect your taxpayer rights. We can offer you help if your tax problem is causing a hardship, or you've tried but haven't been able to resolve your problem with the IRS. If you qualify for our assistance, which is always free, we will do everything possible to help you. Visit www.taxpayeradvocate.irs.gov or call 1-877-777-4778.

Tax Information: The IRS provides the following sources for forms, publications, and additional information. • Tax Questions: 1-800-829-1040 (1-800-829-4059 for TTY/TDD) • Forms and Publications: 1-800-829-3676 (1-800-829-4059 for TTY/TDD) • Internet: www.irs.gov • Small Business Ombudsman: A small business entity can participate in the regulatory process and comment on enforcement actions of the IRS by calling 1-888-REG-FAIR. • Treasury Inspector General for Tax Administration: You can condentially report misconduct, waste, fraud, or abuse by an IRS employee by calling 1-800-366-4484 (1-800-877-8339 for TTY/TDD). You can remain anonymous.

NINE COMMON FILING ERRORS TO AVOID
ACCORDING TO IRS.GOV

IRS Tax Tip 2017-24, March 6, 2017

The IRS encourages taxpayers to file an accurate tax return. If a taxpayer makes an error on their return, it will likely take longer for the IRS to process it. This could delay a refund. Avoid many common errors by filing electronically. IRS e-file is the most accurate way to file a tax return. All taxpayers can use IRS Free File at no cost.

Here are nine common errors to avoid when preparing a tax return:

Missing or Inaccurate Social Security Numbers. Be sure to enter each SSN on a tax return exactly as printed on the Social Security card.

Misspelled Names. Spell all names listed on a tax return exactly as listed on that individual's Social Security card.

Filing Status Errors. Some people claim the wrong filing status, such as Head of Household instead of Single. The Interactive Tax Assistant on IRS.gov can help taxpayers choose the correct status. E-file software also helps prevent mistakes.

Math Mistakes. Math errors are common. They range from simple addition and subtraction to more complex items.

Transactions like figuring the taxable portion of a pension, IRA distribution or Social Security benefits are more difficult and result in more errors. Taxpayers should always double check their math. Better yet, tax preparation software does it automatically, so file electronically.

Errors in Figuring Tax Credits or Deductions. Filers can make mistakes figuring their Earned Income Tax Credit, Child and Dependent Care Credit, the standard deduction and other items. Taxpayers need to follow the instructions carefully. For example, if a taxpayer is age 65 or older, or blind, they should be sure to claim the correct, higher standard deduction. The IRS Interactive Tax Assistant can help determine if a taxpayer is eligible for tax credits or deductions.

Incorrect Bank Account Numbers. The IRS strongly urges all taxpayers who have a refund due to choose direct deposit. It's easy and convenient. Be careful to use the right routing and account numbers on the tax return. The fastest and safest way to get a refund is to combine e-file with direct deposit.

Forms Not Signed. An unsigned tax return is like an unsigned check – it's not valid. Both spouses must sign a joint return. Taxpayers can avoid this error by filing their return electronically. Sign an e-filed tax return digitally before sending it to the IRS.

Electronic Filing PIN Errors. When e-filing, the taxpayer signs and validates the tax return electronically with a prior-year Self-

Select Personal Identification Number. If they do not have or know their PIN, they should enter the Adjusted Gross Income from their 2015 tax return originally filed with the IRS. Taxpayers should keep a copy of their tax return.

Beginning in 2017, taxpayers using a software product for the first time may need their Adjusted Gross Income (AGI) amount from their prior-year tax return to verify their identity. Taxpayers can learn more about how to verify their identity and electronically sign tax returns at Validating Your Electronically Filed Tax Return. Do not use the AGI amount from an amended return or a return that the IRS corrected.

Filing with an expired ITIN. A tax return filed with an expired Individual Tax Identification Number (ITIN) will be processed and treated as timely filed, but will be processed without any exemptions or credits claimed. Taxpayers will receive a notice from the IRS explaining that an ITIN must be current before any refund is paid. Once the ITIN is renewed, exemptions and credits are processed and any allowed refund paid. ITIN expiration and renewal information is available on IRS.gov.

IRS DIRTY DOZEN TAX SCAMS

Phishing: Taxpayers need to be on guard against fake emails or websites looking to steal personal information. The IRS will never initiate contact with taxpayers via email about a bill or refund. Don't click on one claiming to be from the IRS. Be wary of emails and websites that may be nothing more than scams to steal personal information. (IR-2017-15)

Phone Scams: Phone calls from criminals impersonating IRS agents remain an ongoing threat to taxpayers. The IRS has seen a surge of these phone scams in recent years as con artists threaten taxpayers with police arrest, deportation and license revocation, among other things. (IR-2017-19)

Identity Theft: Taxpayers need to watch out for identity theft especially around tax time. The IRS continues to aggressively pursue the criminals that file fraudulent returns using someone else's Social Security number. Though the agency is making progress on this front, taxpayers still need to be extremely cautious and do everything they can to avoid being victimized. (IR-2017-22)

Return Preparer Fraud: Be on the lookout for unscrupulous return preparers. The vast majority of tax professionals provide honest, high-quality service. There are some dishonest preparers who set up shop each filing season to perpetrate refund fraud, identity theft, and other scams that hurt taxpayers. (IR-2017-23)

Fake Charities: Be on guard against groups masquerading as charitable organizations to attract donations from unsuspecting contributors. Be wary of charities with names similar to familiar or nationally known organizations. Contributors should take a few extra minutes to ensure their hard-earned money goes to legitimate and currently eligible charities. IRS.gov has the tools taxpayers need to check out the status of charitable organizations. (IR-2017-25)

Inflated Refund Claims: Taxpayers should be on the lookout for anyone promising inflated refunds. Be wary of anyone who asks taxpayers to sign a blank return, promises a big refund before looking at their records or charges fees based on a percentage of the refund. Fraudsters use flyers, advertisements, phony storefronts and word of mouth via community groups where trust is high to find victims. (IR-2017-26)

Excessive Claims for Business Credits: Avoid improperly claiming the fuel tax credit, a tax benefit generally not available to most taxpayers. The credit is usually limited to off-highway business use, including use in farming. Taxpayers should also avoid misuse of the research credit. Improper claims often involve failures to participate in or substantiate qualified research activities and/or satisfy the requirements related to qualified research expenses. (IR-2017-27)

Falsely Padding Deductions on Returns: Taxpayers should avoid the temptation to falsely inflate deductions or expenses on their returns to pay less than what they owe or potentially receive larger refunds. Think twice before overstating deductions such as charitable contributions and business expenses or improperly claiming credits such as the Earned Income Tax Credit or Child Tax Credit. (IR-2017-28)

Falsifying Income to Claim Credits: Don't invent income to erroneously qualify for tax credits, such as the Earned Income Tax Credit. Taxpayers are sometimes talked into doing this by con artists. Taxpayers should file the most accurate return possible because they are legally responsible for what is on their return. This scam can lead to taxpayers facing large bills to pay back taxes, interest and penalties. In some cases, they may even face criminal prosecution. (IR-2017-29)

Abusive Tax Shelters: Don't use abusive tax structures to avoid paying taxes. The IRS is committed to stopping complex tax avoidance schemes and the people who create and sell them. The vast majority of taxpayers pay their fair share, and everyone should be on the lookout for people peddling tax shelters that sound too good to be true. When in doubt, taxpayers should seek an independent opinion regarding complex products they are offered. (IR-2017-31)

Frivolous Tax Arguments: Don't use frivolous tax arguments to avoid paying tax. Promoters of frivolous schemes encourage taxpayers to make unreasonable and outlandish claims even though they have been repeatedly thrown out of court. While taxpayers have the right to contest their tax liabilities in court, no one has the right to disobey the law or disregard their responsibility to pay taxes. The penalty for filing a frivolous tax return is $5,000. (IR-2017-33)

Offshore Tax Avoidance: The recent string of successful enforcement actions against offshore tax cheats and the financial organizations that help them shows that it's a bad bet to hide money and income offshore. Taxpayers are best served by coming in voluntarily and getting caught up on their tax-filing responsibilities. The IRS offers the Offshore Voluntary Disclosure Program to enable people to catch up on their filing and tax obligations. (IR-2017-35)

UNDERSTANDING TAXES RESOLUTION TERMS
Glossary of Terms

Resolving your IRS problems can be frustrating and complicated, but getting the tax help you need doesn't have to be.

Here are some common tax relief terms to help you settle your IRS debt and permanently achieve your tax resolution.

ABATEMENT

A partial or complete cancellation of taxes, penalties or interest owed by a taxpayer. Taxpayers can request that penalties be abated and in many cases, the IRS removes 100% of the penalty. The IRS requires that you have a good reason to request penalty abatement. While IRS procedures for deciding who qualifies for penalty abatement and for what reason seem to differ in each case, the best thing you can do is to request that the IRS abate your penalties by providing the circumstances surrounding your situation.

ACS SEE AUTOMATED COLLECTION SYSTEM.

Appeal A request by a taxpayer who does not agree with an IRS decision. The action of filing an appeal puts the IRS on notice that the taxpayer doesn't agree with the IRS and is seeking a meeting to change the IRS decision. Audits/examination determinations, offers in compromise, installment payment plans, requests for penalty removal, innocent spouse decisions, levies, liens, seizures and just about every type of intrusive action taken by the IRS can be appealed. Also see Collection Appeal Request, Request for a Collection Due Process Hearing, or Application for Taxpayer Assistance Order

APPEAL

A request by a taxpayer who does not agree with an IRS decision. The action of filing an appeal puts the IRS on notice that the taxpayer doesn't agree with the IRS and is seeking a meeting to change the IRS decision. Audits/examination determinations, offers in compromise, installment payment plans, requests for penalty removal, innocent spouse decisions, levies, liens, seizures and just about every type of intrusive action taken by the IRS can be appealed. Also see Collection Appeal Request, Request for a Collection Due Process Hearing, or Application for Taxpayer Assistance Order

APPLICATION FOR TAXPAYER ASSISTANCE ORDER

(Form 911) Type of appeal used when the taxpayer has exhausted all other means of trying to resolve an issue with the IRS but an agreeable decision can not be reached. This appeal is handled by the IRS's Taxpayer Advocate Service. The Taxpayer Advocate Service can not over turn an appeals officer decision. However, they can to expedite matters and are very helpful in most circumstances. Also see Appeal, Collection Appeal Request, or Request for a Collection Due Process Hearing

AUDIT

A tax audit is an examination of the tax return you filed with the IRS. Also see Field & Office Audits or Correspondence Audit

AUTOMATED COLLECTION SYSTEM (ACS)

A computerized collection process for IRS collectors to contact delinquent taxpayers by telephone and mail.

BACK TAXES

IRS debt from taxes owed from a prior year(s). The IRS assesses back taxes when a taxpayer does not pay taxes when they become due, fails to report all income and taxes on a return, or fails to file a return.

BANK LEVY

The IRS can issue a bank levy to take your cash in savings and checking accounts. When the IRS levies a bank account, the levy is only for the particular day the levy is received by the bank. These are generally referred to as "one shot" levies. The bank is required to remove whatever amount is available in your account that day (up to the amount of the IRS levy) and send it to the IRS in 21 days unless notified otherwise by the IRS. This type of levy does not effect any future deposits made into your bank account unless the IRS issues another Bank Account Levy. Also see Levies or Wage Levy.

BANKRUPTCY

Tax debt may be eligible for discharge in bankruptcy. However, bankruptcy does not always remove all tax liabilities as not all IRS taxes, penalties and interest qualify for complete 100% discharge. In order for a taxpayer to benefit from bankruptcy laws, the taxpayer must determine whether or not tax liabilities must are eligible for discharge.

CERTIFIED TAX RESOLUTION SPECIALIST

Tax professional who has met the educational, experience, and examination requirements prescribed by the American Society of Tax Problem Solvers (ASTPS). The CTRS designation is restricted to Enrolled Agents, CPA or Tax Attorney in good standing, who have proven expertise to resolve a wide range of tax problems. The services a CTRS provides to individuals and businesses include securing offers in compromise, installment agreements, penalty abatement, innocent spouse relief, release of liens or levies, non-filer issues and many others. Also see Tax Attorney

COLLATERAL AGREEMENT

An agreement sometimes secured by the IRS prior to acceptance of an Offer in Compromise when the IRS wants to cover a future, reasonably possible event, such as a significant increase in income.

COLLECTION APPEAL REQUEST (CAP FORM 9423)

Type of appeal used when a taxpayer and a Revenue Officer (Collection) do not see eye-to-eye on an intrusive collection tactic that the IRS wants to implement or has already implemented such as a Levy, Lien, seizure or the denial or termination of an installment agreement. Also see Appeal, Request for a Collection Due Process Hearing, or Application for Taxpayer Assistance Order

COLLECTION DIVISION

Tax collectors who work out of the IRS Service Center, Automated Collection or District Office.

COLLECTION INFORMATION STATEMENT (IRS FORMS 433-A, 433-B, AND 433-F)

IRS financial statements that require disclosure of personal information, particularly assets, income and expenses.

CORRESPONDENCE AUDIT

A correspondence audit is done by mail. The IRS sends you a letter either alleging you forgot some item of income or requests to see the documentation to substantiate a deduction you have taken on your tax return. The most common type is the CP2000 notice, a computer generated notice that you failed to report an item of income. These must be checked closely since the reporting agency, often time the Social Security Administration for W2's, can make typographical errors. If you fail to properly dispute these errors the IRS is free to assess and collect the tax they believe is owed. And if ignored long enough, your only recourse is to pay the tax, penalty, and interest and then sue the IRS in court, an expensive proposition.

CURRENT MARKET VALUE

The amount you could reasonably expect to be paid for the asset if you sold it today. You can find out the value from realtors, used car dealers, publications, furniture dealers, or other experts on specific types of assets. You are advised to include a copy of any written estimate with your Collection Information Statement.

DELINQUENT TAX RETURN

A tax return not filed by the due date (April 15) or by the dates allowed through the IRS extension periods (August 15 and October 15). Failure to file tax returns may be construed as a criminal (misdemeanor and potentially a felony!) act by the IRS. This type of criminal act is punishable by one year in jail and $10,000 for each year not filed. Regardless of what you have heard, you have the right to file your original tax return, no matter how late it's filed.

EXAMINATION OFFICIAL

IRS term for a tax audit

EXPENSES NOT GENERALLY ALLOWED

Expenses not allowed such as claim tuition for private schools, public or private college expenses, charitable contributions, voluntary retirement contributions, payments on unsecured debts such as credit card bills, cable television charges and other similar expenses as necessary living expenses. These expenses can be allowed when you can prove that they are necessary for the health and welfare of you or your family or for the production of income.

FAIR MARKET VALUE

The price a willing buyer and seller of property would agree on as fair; neither being under any compulsion to buy or sell and both having reasonable knowledge of relevant facts.

FEDERALLY AUTHORIZED

Only Enrolled Agents CPA's and Attorneys are allowed to represent taxpayers before the IRS. An un-enrolled tax preparer can defend a client for whom he prepared a tax return during audit but cannot take it to appeals or represent the taxpayer before the collections division. Our members are all federally authorized to represent all taxpayers. We are not affiliated with nor are employees of the IRS. We work exclusively to provide you with the best representation possible in your controversies with the IRS.

FIELD & OFFICE AUDITS

Audits are an examination of the tax return you filed with the IRS. The examiner, typically a Revenue Agent, looks for undocumented income and unsubstantiated expenses or deductions. If the audit is performed in the IRS office, it is considered an office audit. These are common for wage earners. If the audit is conducted at the taxpayer's home or place of business, these are field audits. For our clients, field audits are typically conducted in our offices. It is generally too disruptive to have an IRS auditor or examiner hanging around your office for several days.

FREEDOM OF INFORMATION ACT

A federal law giving citizens the right to see governmental documents, including their IRS files. Freedom of Information documents can be used to explain why, how, when and where a taxpayer's IRS problems started. Having this information is helpful as it discloses the IRS information used to assess taxes, penalties and interest against the taxpayer. Any taxpayer having difficulty in sorting out what the IRS is doing to them should consider using the Freedom of Information Act to obtain their IRS files.

FRAUD LOSS RECOVERY

Victims of fraudulent investment schemes (Ponzi Scheme) who have lost all or most of their investment, may be eligible to take advantage the United States Tax Code (law) and recoup 30% to 40% of their losses under Internal Revenue Code Section 165 treatment. Most victims of these types of white collar crimes can convert their capital stock losses into ordinary losses and offset them against prior, current and future ordinary taxable income, thereby reducing the taxes paid in those years, and receiving a refund with interest. The process generally involves amending prior years tax returns and is a highly technical, time consuming and complex process that could prove invaluable to those who've sustained major investment losses due to fraud and white collar crime.

FUTURE INCOME

The amount the IRS could collect from your future income by subtracting necessary living expenses from your monthly income over a set number of months. For a cash offer, you must offer what you could pay in monthly payments over forty-eight months (or the remainder of the ten-year statutory period for collection, whichever is less). For a short-term deferred offer, you must offer what you could pay in monthly payments over sixty months (or the remainder of the statutory period for collection, whichever is less). For a deferred payment offer, you must offer what you could pay in monthly payments during the remaining time we could legally receive payments.

GARNISHMENTS - WAGE GARNISHMENTS

Garnishments are ongoing levies. Most common is the wage garnishment in which the IRS takes all but a pittance of your take home pay. The IRS would serve its garnishment on your employer. The employer is required to leave you a preset amount to live on (although you couldn't live on the amount the IRS authorizes) and send the balance to the IRS toward your tax debt. The garnishment is one of the most effective tools the IRS has to get you to the bargaining table. And most employers hate garnishments since it creates a lot of extra work for their payroll department. Some employers have policies against having unresolved tax debts. We have a strong track record of getting the IRS to release the garnishment. Also see Levies.

INNOCENT SPOUSE

In order to help taxpayers that are being subjected to IRS problems because of their spouse's (or ex-spouses) actions, the IRS has come up with guidelines for tax relief where a person may qualify as an innocent spouse. This means that if a taxpayer can prove they fit in those guidelines, they may not be subject to the taxes caused by their spouses or ex-spouses. They may qualify for innocent spouse tax relief.

INSTALLMENT AGREEMENT

The installment agreement is a payment plan between you and the IRS. The IRS has some flexibility regarding the payment amount as long as the debt will be paid off before the statute of limitations expire. If the amount due is small and you are offering large payments, it can be quite simple to get an installment agreement. The agreement comes with some strings attached, such as staying current on the filing and paying of future tax returns for as long as the agreement is in place. Penalties and interest will continue to be charged although the penalty rate is currently reduced during the installment agreement. The IRS charges a nominal fee to setup an installment agreement. For larger debts or those debts involving payroll tax issues the IRS may elect to assign a Revenue Officer (debt collector) to determine the maximum payment they can bet from you.

JEOPARDY ASSESSMENT

An expedited procedure by which the IRS imposes a tax liability without notifying you first. A jeopardy assessment is rare and used when the IRS believes the taxpayer is about to leave the country or hide assets.

LEVIES

A levy is the taking of an asset. Most common is the bank levy. The IRS serves a levy notice on your bank for money held in your account. The account is frozen for an amount of money up to the amount owed to the IRS. If there is less in the account than you owe, the whole account is frozen for 21 days. During that time the original amount in the account is locked up. Any new money added is not part of the original levy. At the end of the 21 days the money is transferred to the IRS unless you have obtained a release from the IRS. Most levies are one-shot deals but the IRS can continue to get new levies on a daily basis. They generally don't. Part of resolving tax debts is to obtain from the IRS a release of the levy. Also see Bank Levy or Wage Levy.

LIENS

A lien is merely a statement alleging that you owe a tax debt. It is legally created anytime you owe taxes. It can show up on your credit report, and if the IRS locates property you own, it can be filed against the property. The most common example is a lien filed against your home. Once filed, you cannot sell the asset until the lien is paid off. For houses, the payoff is part of closing. And if you don't have sufficient equity to payoff the mortgage(s) and lien, you can only sell your home by bringing your own money to closing.

LIQUIDATION VALUE

The amount the IRS can get from a distress sale of a taxpayer's assets, usually a public auction (typically 70% of fair market value).

LOCAL STANDARDS

Maximum allowances for housing and utilities known as Local Standards, vary by location. Unlike the National Standards, taxpayers are allowed the amount actually spent, or the standard, whichever is less. There are separate allowance amounts for transportation expenses.

NATIONAL STANDARDS

Allowances for food, clothing and other items, known as the National Standards, apply nationwide except for Alaska and Hawaii, which have their own tables. Taxpayers are allowed the total National Standards amount for their family size and income level, without questioning amounts actually spent.

NECESSARY EXPENSES

The allowable payments you make to support you and your family's health and welfare and/or the production of income. This expense allowance does not apply to business entities. Publication 1854, How to Prepare a Collection Information Statement (Form 433-A), explains the National Standard Expenses and gives the allowable amounts. We derive these amounts from the Bureau of Labor Statistics (BLS) Consumer Expenditure Survey. We also use information from the Bureau of the Census to determine local expenses for housing, utilities, and transportation. Note: If the IRS determines that the facts and circumstances of your situation indicate that using the scheduled allowance of necessary expenses is inadequate, we will allow you an adequate means for providing basic living expenses. However, you must provide documentation that supports a determination that using national and local expense standards leaves you an inadequate means of providing for basic living expenses.

NOTICE OF DEFICIENCY

An IRS notice informing a taxpayer that he or she owes the IRS the amount listed, which is the excess of the taxpayer's correct tax liability for the taxable year over the amount of taxes already paid for such year.

NTPI FELLOW®

This designation is evidence of significant expertise in the representation of taxpayers before the IRS. Becoming an NTPI Fellow isn't easy. To fully appreciate what it says about your tax professional, here's a rundown of the prerequisites and requirements to achieve this distinction.

In order to enroll in the National Tax Practice Institute (NTPI), your tax professional must be an enrolled agent*, CPA or attorney. These are the only three professional groups that have full rights of representation before IRS. That means that not only can they speak directly to the IRS regarding your taxes without you being present, they can represent you in an IRS audit, collection or appeal. If you find yourself in tax trouble, you'll want one of these professionals by your side.

NTPI Fellows have completed a stringent, three-level program of study that covers all facets of representing clients before the IRS. They have learned to guide their clients through the often challenging maze of IRS codes, internal regulations and agency structure.

OFFER IN COMPROMISE (OIC)

The "pennies on the dollar" program allows taxpayers to settle their tax debt for something less than full payment. The criteria is fairly rigid and was designed by Congress, not the IRS. It is a pure business decision. The IRS determines what it could liquidate you for and adds to that what it could collect over the next 48 months and arrives at a minimum amount it might accept. The OIC program is a great program for those that qualify. But don't use it lightly since it stops the running of the statute of limitations on collections. Proper preparation of IRS financial statements is the key to a good OIC. And since the IRS is back-logged with Offers, patience is a virtue. But for those that qualify, this is a great program. Offers can be made with a lump sum payment or payments over time (much like an installment agreement). Acceptance by the IRS of an offer does come with strings attached, such as staying current with filing and paying for five years after the offer is accepted.

OFFSHORE TAX EVASION DEFENSE

If you have undeclared funds in foreign bank accounts, now is the time to act in order to reduce your chances of criminal prosecution, minimize severe IRS penalties and work out a structured IRS payment plan. If you believe that you owe back taxes on your foreign accounts, you will need expert tax help (specialized tax attorney, tax resolution firm, etc.) disclosing your foreign funds, obtaining FBAR compliance, and mounting your offshore tax evasion defense.

PAYROLL TAX PROBLEMS

If you owe delinquent payroll taxes, it is important to know that the IRS assigns a higher priority to collecting employment taxes than income taxes. Delinquent payroll taxes will not only generate huge IRS penalties and debt, but may also be considered a federal crime. It is important to resolve payroll tax debt problems swiftly to protect the future of your company.

PAYMENT PLANS

See Installment Agreement.

PENALTIES

The IRS assesses two types of penalties on late filed income tax returns. The first and most expensive is the failure to file. Any tax return filed after the due date, including extensions, is considered late. The penalty is based upon the balance due with the tax return. The second penalty is the failure to pay. This is also based upon the amount due with the tax return and is calculated from the due date of the return, without regard to extensions. Some people erroneously believe that since they have a refund they don't need to worry about filing on time. However, if the return is ever audited and the result is a balance due, the penalties will be based upon the due date of the return, even if the audit occurs 2 years later.

PENDING OFFER

An offer pending starting with the date an authorized IRS official signs Form 656 and accepts your waiver of the statutory period of limitation, and remains pending until an authorized IRS official accepts, rejects or acknowledges withdrawal of the offer in writing.

PETITION

A form filed with the U.S. Tax Court requesting a hearing to contest a proposed IRS tax assessment.

POWER OF ATTORNEY (IRS FORM 2848)

A form appointing a tax representative to deal with the IRS on your behalf.

PROTRACTED INSTALLMENT AGREEMENT

An installment agreement that extends beyond the period allowed under IRS issued guidelines.

QUICK SALE VALUE

The amount that can be realized from the sale of a taxpayer's assets when financial and other pressures force the taxpayer to sell quickly, typically in ninety days or less. This amount generally is less than current value, but may be equal to or higher, based on local circumstances typically 80% of fair market value.

REALIZABLE VALUE

The quick sale value amount minus what you owe to a secured creditor. The creditor must have priority over a filed Notice of Federal Tax Lien before we allow a subtraction from the asset's value.

REASONABLE CAUSE

There are a variety of reasons why taxpayers don't file or pay. Divorce, job loss, death of family members, mental or physical diseases, drug and alcohol problems, dog ate the homework, etc. are many of the reasons why taxpayers fail to file or pay. The law allows for the abatement (removal) of penalties for reasonable cause. Obviously, it is very subjective.

REASONABLE COLLECTION POTENTIAL (RCP)

The total realizable value of your assets plus your future income. The total is generally your minimum offer amount.

RECONSIDERATION

Audit reconsiderations are discretionary on the part of the IRS. However, we have been successful in convincing the IRS to reopen an audit where the taxpayers were poorly represented or new information is now available that was not available at the original audit.

REQUEST FOR A COLLECTION DUE PROCESS HEARING (CDP FORM 12153)

An all purpose appeal that generally is invoked by filing form 12153, when the IRS has already issued a Lien, is about to issue a levy, and you want to request an alternative collection option that is less intrusive such as an Offer in Compromise, Payment Plan, be declared currently not collectible, request Innocent Spouse Relief, or request a withdrawal, discharge or subordination of a lien. There are certain legal and administrative notices and requirements the IRS must send/meet before a taxpayer can file this type of Appeal. Also see Appeal, Collection Appeal Request or Application for Taxpayer Assistance Order

RUNNING OUT

The IRS has 10 years to collect on back taxes unless the time period has been extended, either by consent of the taxpayer or by certain actions of the taxpayer. The most common reason for the statute of limitations to collect to have been extended is when the IRS has no ability to collect on the debt. Typically, this is because the taxpayer was out of the country, had made an Offer in Compromise, or was under the bankruptcy court. During the time the IRS could not legally collect the running of the 10-year statute of limitations is stopped (tolled). Knowing what has happened during the 10 years is critical to knowing when the IRS can no longer dun you for the debt. It is not uncommon for a tax debt to be removed because the time to collect has expired. The IRS is allowed to accept payments from you but they can't dun you for any debt that is outside the statute of limitations for collections.

STATUTE OF LIMITATION

Legal limits imposed on the IRS for assessing and collecting taxes, and on the Justice Department for charging taxpayers with tax crimes. The current statute of limitation for collection is 10 years from the date of assessment. However, the statute can be extended by certain actions of the taxpayer.

SUBSTITUTE FOR RETURN (SFR)

The law allows the IRS to take the income reported to it under your social security number and file a tax return for you. If you were single the prior year, they will file you as single. If you were married the prior year, they will file a return for you as married filing separate. They will not take any itemized deductions you might be legible for nor will they deduct for any dependents you might be entitled for. It will be a very basic return designed to produce the highest amount of tax allowed to the IRS. It is rarely in your best interest. And since you didn't file the return yourself, the year remains open (subject to assessment and collection) forever.

TAX ATTORNEY

An attorney that specializes in providing tax relief to individuals and businesses with tax problems at the state or federal level. A tax attorney can help taxpayers secure offers in compromise, installment agreements, penalty abatement, innocent spouse relief, release of liens or levies, non-filer issues and many other tax settlements. Also see Certified Tax Resolution Specialist (CTRS)

TAX DEBT RELIEF/ TAX RELIEF

Assistance for tax-burdened individuals or businesses who seek a reduction in the amount of taxes owed. Tax relief includes settlements obtained by offers in compromise, installment agreements, penalty abatement, innocent spouse relief, release of liens or levies and other tax resolution strategies.

TAX HELP

While taxpayers may always represent themselves before the IRS.

many taxpayers find dealing with the IRS frustrating, time-consuming, intimidating or all of the above and so they make the decision to hire professional tax help (specialized tax attorney, tax resolution firm, etc.) to negotiate with the IRS on their behalf.

TAXPAYER ADVOCATE SERVICE

An IRS program that provides an independent system to assure that unresolved problems are promptly and fairly handled.

TRUST FUND RECOVERY

Penalty (formerly called 100-percent Penalty) A penalty incurred by the responsible person(s) of a business for failure to pay Withholding and Federal Insurance Contributions Act Taxes (Social Security taxes)

UNCOLLECTIBLE

A temporary designation by the IRS meaning a taxpayer does not have significant assets or available income, at the present time, from which to satisfy an IRS debt in part or in full. This designation takes a case out of collection, until a taxpayer has an ability to pay.

VOLUNTARY DISCLOSURE

Taxpayers can participate in the voluntary disclosure program before the IRS has initiated a civil or criminal examination or before the taxpayer has received notice of such an investigation.

The IRS offers leniency for voluntary disclosure and it is good advice for any American with IRS tax problems to take advantage of this policy. Under this policy, taxpayers have avoided prosecution for possible tax evasion and have had taxes, penalties, and interest reduced.

WAIVER

Voluntarily surrendering a legal right, such as the right to have the IRS collection period on a delinquent tax debt expire at the end of the statutory time period. The IRS may require waivers in exchange.

WAGE LEVY

The IRS can levy your wages or accounts receivable and all other sources of income. The person, company, or institution that is served the levy must comply. If they do not comply, they too may have daunting IRS (legal) problems. Wage levies are filed with your employer and remain in effect until the IRS notifies the employer that the wage levy has been released. These are generally referred to as a continuous levy. Most wage levies take so much money from the taxpayer's paycheck that the taxpayer doesn't have enough money to live on. Also see Bank Levy or Levies.

If You Have A Tax Problem And You Want to Contact Carlos Samaniego, EA for assistance for your Tax Problems. You can contact him at 909.570.1103. Be prepared to leave a message.

If you would like to book an appointment with Carlos go to

TaxDebtConsultant.com